EXTREME
ADVENTURE
EXPERIENCING THE WORD OF GOD

EXTREME
ADVENTURE
EXPERIENCING THE WORD OF GOD

TERROL W. JONES

BAKER TRITTIN PRESS

Winona Lake, Indiana

Extreme Adventure, Experiencing the Word of God
By Terrol W. Jones

Scriptures taken from the New King James Version. Copyright © 1982 by Thomas Nelson, Inc. Used by permission. All rights reserved. Other versions will be noted whenever used.

Printed in the United States of America
Cover Art: Fusion Hill
Published by Baker Trittin Press
P.O. Box 277
Winona Lake, Indiana 46590

To order additional copies please call (888) 741-4386
or email info@btconcepts.com
http://www.bakertrittinpress.com

Publishers Cataloging-Publication Data
Terrol W. Jones, 1943-
        Extreme Adventure, Experiencing the Word of God/
        Terrol W. Jones - Winona Lake, Indiana
        Baker Trittin Press, 2007

            p.   cm.

Library of Congress Control Number: 2007920782
ISBN 10: 0-9787316-2-X
ISBN 13: 978-0-9787316-2-5
        1. Autobiography 2. Religious 3. Christian
        I. Title   II. Extreme Adventure, Experiencing the
        Word of God
BIO18000

DEDICATION

In loving memory of Andrew Christian Surace who left us far too early. This book is dedicated to his brothers and sisters, to our sons Nathan and Timothy, to the youth and young adults of Cape May County, New Jersey, and throughout North America. May they find reality in living for Jesus Christ and experience the Extreme Adventure of being His disciples from the Garden State to the Lone Star State and into the entire world.

ACKNOWLEDGEMENTS

When I began writing this testimonial, I questioned whether personal names should be mentioned. Undoubtedly some influential people would be unintentionally overlooked. Others in India and Sri Lanka might be put in jeopardy, so in some cases I did not use the real names. We must recognize the prayer partners and supporters who have stood by us, some for nearly forty years. Without them we would not have been able to accomplish our mission on Earth. A special thanks to all of you who receive our monthly "I AM" newsletters and remember us faithfully in prayer and giving. Many names have been lost in the recesses of my mind, but that does not make them any less important.

God knows the faithful Sunday School teachers at Main Street United Methodist Church who planted seeds of faith in my heart. My Father and Mother, George and Rosie, gave me life and a stable, loving home in which my brothers Steve and Michael, and sisters Pattie and Joanna were raised.

Pastors and teachers nurtured faith in my heart and challenged me to a deeper understanding of life so that I, myself, answered the call of God to be a school teacher and minister of His Word. Some of these pastors, teachers, writers, missionaries, and professors are referred to in this book but not all by any means. It would have been a cumbersome task to mention everyone who has had significant influence on my life.

I appreciate the initial editing done by my dear help-mate, Pattie, and then by Pastor Traci Nessler, and my niece, Amy O'Connell. Ellen Varughese also gave me helpful advice. Kasey Hatzung designed the book cover with some ideas from our son, Nathan. Joanne McNeely created and continues to up-date our website for which we are very thankful. The sketches by my nephew, Richie Tornetta helped me to visualize the chapter themes. Our good friend, Joe Acosta, patiently snapped photos, one of which is included on the back cover. Bob and Judy Worrell made the first printing possible with their generous initial gift which was followed by gifts from others who also believed in this project. Thank you for your support and confidence in us.

Pattie and I are also thankful for Pastor Andy Surace and Covenant Life Christian Fellowship of Seaville, New Jersey, for the privilege of serving them and for their continued missionary support.

I would like to thank Wayne Pence who recommended Baker Trittin Press as a possible publisher of this book. Thanks to Dr. Marvin Baker and Paul Trittin for accepting this first time author's work. Their help in preparing the book for print has been a great blessing.

Finally but not least of all we are exceedingly thankful for our Asian family that has loved us over the years and adopted us. In India and Sri Lanka, especially, we feel so very much at home. Our lives have become a beautiful tapestry with the people there. Only eternity will reveal the whole story.

Unless otherwise noted, all Scripture references are taken from the New King James Version of the Bible.

TABLE OF CONTENTS

FOREWORDS

Terry Jones is another example of someone going short-term into missions and staying for life. His story needs to be told and now, here it is!

India, with over one billion people, has many states with less than 1% who follow Christ. India needs to get much more attention from the church around the world. Reading this book and sharing it with others will be a great help in the super-human task that we face there.

My heart breaks when I hear all the negatives about sending American, British, German and other so-called 'western' missionaries. The truth is that we need people like Terry and Pattie, no matter what their nationality. Let's remember that people look at outward appearances, but God looks on the heart.

At least 20% of the people in the world have never heard or read the Gospel. Just hearing it once is never enough.

I hope this book will inspire some to go and all to pray and give.

George Verwer, Co-Founder, Operation Mobilization
London, U.K.

As a native missionary in India, I travel often by train. A month ago, I was on a trip that lasted three days and three nights. I hadn't eaten for two days, and I was very exhausted. At the same time I felt a certain excitement as the train was slowly creeping to my destination station. I had already gathered my bags and was standing at the open train door, holding on to a steel bar, scanning the crowd for a familiar face. I didn't know who would meet me.

As the crowded platform came into view, my eyes suddenly fell on my tall, American friend, Terry Jones, off in the distance. I shouted, "Hallelujah!" and he shouted back, "Hallelujah!" from across the crowded platform. I thought, *What is Terry doing here?* It was a complete surprise. I had met with Terry and Pattie Jones just a month earlier in Kansas. Now they were in India meeting my train.

This is what Terry is all about. He is a man of action. He turns up in the most unusual places, always willing to help. He and his wife, Pattie, have blessed scores of brothers and sisters especially in India and Sri Lanka. Without their support I would never be where I am today.

Whoever reads this book, please understand that it took about thirty-five years of hard work, sacrifice, and preparation to write. Terry never held anything back for himself but gave it all.

Yesterday an American missionary spoke in my church. I wept during the whole service as she spoke about what the Lord is doing in Africa. I believe God still uses western missionaries in the third world countries. Terry is living proof of this truth.

Terry is one of a kind. I believe it will be a blessing for you to invite him and his wife to speak in your church or fellowship group if you wish. I promise they will be a blessing for you and your people.

N.J. Varughese
All India Mission, President
Jharkand (Bihar), North India
May 2006

I am crucified with Christ: nevertheless I live; yet not I, but Christ livith in me: and the life which I now live in the flesh I live by faith of the Son of God, who loved me, and gave himself for me.

Galatians 2:20 KJV

Because of the increase of wickedness (lawlessness or terrorism) the love of most will grow cold, but he who stands firm to the end will be saved. And this gospel of the kingdom will be preached in the whole world as a testimony to all nations, and then the end will come.

Matthew 24:12-14 NIV (author's words in parenthesis)

If anyone desires to come after Me, let him deny himself, and take up his cross daily, and follow Me. For whoever desires to save his life will lose it, but whoever loses his life for My sake will save it.

Luke 9:23-24 NKJV

After this I looked and there before me was a great multitude that no one could count, from every nation, tribe, people and language, standing before the throne and in front of the Lamb. They were wearing white robes and were holding palm branches in their hands. And they cried out in a loud voice: 'Salvation belongs to our God, who sits on the throne, and to the Lamb.'

Revelation 7:9-10 NIV

PROLOGUE

Reading *The Purpose Driven Life* by Pastor Rick Warren in early 2005, my heart soared. Pastor Rick described so succinctly what we have been living for many years. The information was not new, but his message clarified and authenticated my life's focus. As I read, I felt like a classical guitar being plucked and strummed by Segovia.

I had been writing for many years. An unfinished book was always stored away in a dresser drawer. I would add to it when I got an inspirational thought and then stop with the proverbial writer's block. However, I was pregnant with a message in my spirit. I had been with my wife Pattie in the delivery room when Nathan and Timmy both made their grand appearances at Lakeside Medical Center in Kandy, Sri Lanka, in 1981 and 1983 respectively. Laboring to give birth is not an easy task. At the point of Nathan's appearance, Pattie let out a chilling scream. Through the white gossamer, surgical mask, Dr. Ramalingam amusingly muffled, "Pattie, the Concorde jet has nothing over you."

A similar shout came from my mouth with the end of the final chapter of this book. It was a victory shout. This book has been a long time in coming but it is here. Now comes the distribution challenge. I had read the manuscript for the book, *Holy Sex,* by our dear friend, Pastor Terry Wier. I was convinced that his book would be the catalyst used by God to destroy Satan's stronghold in the area of sexuality, especially in the United States. Unfortunately the one million dollars originally offered to market it was withdrawn. Now it sits comparatively unnoticed on the racks of Barnes & Noble and Borders bookstores. Still I have hope that it will be resurrected from the shelves and thrust into the public's notice. It's message is desperately needed especially in the Church at this hour.

On the contrary, I had no pending offer to market my book, but I do have a fire within me to spread the message, summoning our younger generations to experience the extreme adventure of walking with Christ. It is a challenge to actually do something incredibly real, ultimately satisfying and daring! This book is all about a relationship, a dynamic friendship with the Creator God and the Lord Jesus Christ. There is no religion here. There are no spooky, Hollywood-type, special effects or flowery histrionics. Following the Lord and being committed to the Kingdom of God on Earth as it is in Heaven is not an imaginary mind game. The Word of God is an amazingly practical book. It works!

Years ago I highlighted a sentence in Watchman Nee's book, *The Spiritual Man*. It represents the main thesis for *Extreme Adventure*. This great Chinese Christian wrote,

> *Genuine spiritual knowledge lies not in wonderful and mysterious thoughts but in actual spiritual experience through union of the believer's life with truth.*

It is imperative that you keep that statement in mind as you read through this book. I have used different translations of the Bible just as Pastor Rick Warren did in his best seller. You will benefit most if you have your preferred Bible translation in hand for quick reference. If you are unfamiliar with the Bible, use the Table of Contents section in the front of your Bible. It will take you longer to read my saga, but your understanding of the Word will be greatly enhanced. I hope this will be the journey of a lifetime as you embark on this EXTREME ADVENTURE yourself. The Holy Spirit, Promise of the Father, will lead you.

Chapter
1

RAT IN THE WALL

It was a hot, sultry Calcutta evening in northeast India in 1968. My body had not yet adjusted to the tropical climate, and I was constantly tired and lethargic. That was before I learned to drink lots of water to keep my energy level up. Sleep was much sweeter after learning that, but this night was different. We were a team of Operation Mobilization (OM) fresh recruits preparing to bed down for the night at 16 Beniapukur Road in the old colonial city of Calcutta.

The one hundred year old, gabled house was both the OM regional office and book depot located off Lower Circular Road within walking distance of the Abundant Life Assembly of God where Mark Buntain was pastor. OM enjoyed this great missionary's friendship and support. In the old house on Beniapukur Road there were thousands of books stacked on shelves from floor to ceiling and wall to wall. It was very close quarters, but each of the ten recruits managed to find a niche in which to sleep.

OM is an international Christian training organization which emphasizes Christian literature distribution and world evangelism. In those days they had bases throughout India, and it's many volunteers were divided into Gospel outreach teams. Our Indian teams consisted mostly of nationals from the southern states of Kerala or Tamil Nadu because that is where most Christians live. We new arrivals had crossed the English Channel by ferry and then drove overland from France through Europe, Turkey, Iran, Afghanistan, and then down through the Kyber Pass into Pakistan, before arriving in New Delhi, India, 21 days after leaving England. We then drove on for another nine hundred miles or so to Calcutta. Our transcontinental journey was unquestionably an education and extreme adventure in itself.

That night I found a narrow space between the shelves and rolled out my green, Coleman sleeping bag. The Indian brothers had something equivalent which they simply called a bedroll. My sleep that night was sporadic. A persistent background noise periodically awakened me. It was just loud enough to be irritating. Finally after placing my ear to the wall near my head I realized it was coming from inside. Rats!

Several nights later it was too hot to sleep inside so we camped out on the little lawn in the garden. About midnight I was awakened by something that suddenly brushed by my bag. It looked like an opossum, but on looking closer I realized it was a giant Calcutta sewer rat. Nasty nocturnal vermin! It was an omen. I was about to launch a two-year adventure that would dramatically change my life.

"Upon what does your happiness depend?" That is a question we were asked during our month-long OM orientation in England. Struggling with the answer, my life in India became like a house built on stilts and then cut down. All my senses were assaulted. India was a good place for an American boy from the Midwest to experience culture shock and learn new priorities for living. I would never be the same again!

That rat in the wall meant something more than an irritating sleep disruption. I remembered it and the hole in the wall, symbolically as a problem common to mankind – a gnawing sense of emptiness or incompleteness. Blaise Pascal, the famous French scientist and philosopher, made the claim that inside man is a God-shaped vacuum that can only be filled by God through Jesus Christ.

I soon discovered that India has more religion than any other country in the world, having an estimated 330 million gods! My spiritual eyes were opened during those first two years. I saw the utter depravity of man in this complex country. At the same time the faith of my Indian brothers was in great contrast to the darkness that surrounded them. The reality of Philippians 2:14-15 was evident in their lives.

> Do everything without complaining or arguing, so that you may become blameless and pure, children of God without fault in a crooked and depraved generation, in which you shine like stars in the universe.

I was amazed at the personal testimonies of my newfound Indian friends and teammates. Each one had experienced a haunting emptiness without Jesus Christ – a personal 'rat in the wall' feeling before experiencing his own salvation in Jesus.

After celebrating Christmas together at Beniapukur Road, an Indian brother, A. Stephen, and I were chosen for a special mission in the state of Orissa just south of Calcutta. We traveled by overnight train from Howrah Station through the state of Bengal, arriving in Cuttack the next day.

The train was so crowded the only space available was the floor just outside the toilet. Fortunately it was adjacent to a heavy side door which we propped open throughout the night allowing the putrid urine smell to dissipate a bit with the rush of outside air.

Stephen was raised in one of the 630,000 isolated villages of India, a country often called Hindustan or place of the Hindus. His father was a Hindu priest, and he grew up never having seen a church. Jesus Christ and the Bible were completely unknown to him.

During our journey he related his story, telling how as a young teenager he became restless with the life he felt trapped in. He began to smoke at 13 and got into mischief like riding the train without a ticket and running out of restaurants without paying for his meal. His conscience began to bother him though he did not know what it was at the time. He thought his father would be able to help, so he confided in him.

Addressing him by his Hindu name, his father reassured him. "Arundagam, Son, we will sacrifice a goat to the gods. Everything will be all right." Stephen stood in front of the stone god as his priest father poured the goat's blood and cow's milk on the idol and chanted some incantations. "But the stone god never spoke to my heart," Stephen said. "I did not feel any different." He left the ceremony discouraged and unfulfilled.

That very night in desperation he stole money from his father's temple and set off on a type of pilgrimage searching for answers. *What is this gnawing emptiness I feel?* he wondered. His quest led him to many famous temples where India's holy men keep their vigils and give advice, but he was deeply disappointed. They had no answers for him.

A month later he returned home completely disappointed and with one resolve. He would commit suicide because he was empty and without hope. With money in his pocket he approached the village shop that sold rat poison. When the owner refused to sell it to him, Stephen got angry and shouted, "I have the money, so why don't you let me buy it?"

"Bring your father, and I will sell you the poison." The cautious shopkeeper must have sensed his turmoil.

By this time he was even more determined. *There is no reason to keep on living*, he thought. Returning home he found the rope used to tie their cow to a coconut tree, picked it up, and headed for the shed behind his house. Once inside he positioned the milk stool under the bamboo rafters. Standing on it, he tossed the rope over a rafter, and tied it securely around his neck.

In heart-wrenching agony he cried out, "I searched for you, but I could not find you! Now I am going to die, and I do not know where I am going!" As he lowered his head with tears streaming down his face, he heard an audible voice. Stephen told me that it was the most beautiful, melodious voice you could imagine. "There is a peace for you, my son. There is a peace for you."

That was it. That was all he heard. He saw nothing. Reaching into his pocket he grasped his pocketknife and cut the rope. Jumping to the ground he stumbled to the window to see who had spoken. The moon's glow shimmered silently on the surrounding grove. No one was there.

Stephen, still very much perplexed, began to walk. Through the rows of coconut trees, up the ditch, and onto the dirt road, he trudged along in frustration and confusion. *Who was that voice?* Stephen pondered. After a few miles a young man walked up beside him and asked, "Why do you look so sad?"

"It's none of your concern," Stephen blurted.

"No, but I want to help you," assured the stranger.

Stephen told a portion of his sad story. The young stranger listened intently then spoke, "Believe in Jesus Christ. He died to take away your sins. God raised him from the dead and He is alive today. He will come into you and give you peace right now. Just ask Him to forgive you and receive Him as your Savior."

I was absorbed in Stephen's story but also mesmerized by the continuous click-e-t-clack-click-e-t-clack of the train as it chugged along. The cool early morning air whizzed through the doorway and across our makeshift bed next to the toilet. We adjusted a blanket over us as he continued.

Stephen had never heard the name Jesus. "I have searched all over India for the truth. We have so many gods, but you speak only of Jesus? How can he help me?"

Boldly the young man declared, "Ask Jesus to forgive you and come into you right now. If nothing happens, you have lost nothing. You can go ahead and kill yourself."

Kneeling there on the dusty, moonlit road, Stephen repeated the prayer, "Forgive me Lord. Thank you for dying for me and living again. I believe in you and receive you as my Lord and Savior."

Immediately Stephen felt something. He felt lighter. It was like heavy weights were lifted from his shoulders. Rising from his knees, joy flooded his heart. He was filled with peace and hope. Stephen never saw that young man again. Elated he walked, ran, and skipped until he reached his village. When he told his mother what happened, she got a broom from a corner of the room and began hitting him over the head. "This is not our religion! It is a western foreign religion!" She screamed hysterically.

In the months that followed, circumstances made it unbearable to stay with his family. He was blamed when a poisonous snake bit his mother. Then the stigma of her brother becoming a Christian caused his only sister to think that no one would marry her. She ingested a lethal dose of pesticide. She thought the family line had been corrupted and there was no reason to live. His brothers pinned him against a wall. With a knife pressed to his throat, they threatened to kill him if he did not give up this Jesus god.

The night he left home he had only the clothes he was wearing. He never returned. As he made a bed of banana leaves in the jungle, God placed this scripture in his heart: *When my father and my mother forsake me, Then the LORD will take care of me* (Psalm 27:10).

Stephen was one of the many I met who had experienced 'the rat in the wall,' the gnawing emptiness that eventually led them to a personal salvation experience with the resurrected Jesus Christ. *He who has the Son has life; he who does not have the Son of God does not have life* (I John 5:12).

Stephen's testimony captivated me as we lay side-by-side on the grimy floor. Occasionally we stopped at stations between Howrah in Calcutta and Cuttack, Orissa. At each stop Stephen would pause in his story. Without the wind whizzing over us the urine stench on the train was nauseating. We would walk outside beside the train, stretch, and buy something from a platform vendor – anything to escape the smell.

We hopped onboard again as the car started to move and once more claimed our space outside the latrine. Besides the brisk, early morning breezes we thoroughly enjoyed the hot milk tea which was announced dramatically throughout the night by vendors riding between local stations. They got maximum impact and attention dragging out the words in ever deepening tones. *"Chaiiiiiii Chaiiiii Gutum Dood Chaiiii."* From then on Stephen was to become one of my closest Indian friends. His story caused me to think more deeply about the uniqueness of Jesus Christ.

Sleep proved sporadic. The night was long but finally the stars faded into shades of dawn. The constant clanging of iron wheels across railroad ties changed to a hollow sound, ker-plunk-ker-plunk-ker-plunk. We were on a vast iron trestle. The train slowed slightly, but it was taking a long time to traverse the bridge. *Must be the Mohanadi River*, I thought.

Some twenty years later our dear Brother Vijay Das was miraculously saved from a suicide jump from a similar bridge also located in Orissa. His story is just as dramatic as Stephen's. His life would have ended then and there except for divine intervention. "No other explanation is imaginable," Vijay admitted one afternoon as I sat playing with his pet monkey. We were sitting by the well for the church he had pioneered.

It was in Daltonganj, Jharkand, located in the western part of the state that was formerly called Bihar. This area is crowded with fanatical Hindus, and there has been strong resistance to Christianity. Vijay came to this district with the vision to plant a church. He persevered over the years, and now they have a beautiful church building that was constructed in a field formerly infested by snakes. Today there is a thriving congregation.

That day I preached to a packed church of 200 people. Many walked several miles for the special meetings. The altar area was cluttered with bottles of all sizes and shapes carried to the church. They were filled with different kinds of oils. The villagers had faith that if we prayed over the bottles they could take the healing anointing oil back with them to their villages and pray for others to be healed – and they often were.

Vijay was a missionary here. He had come from the neighboring state of Orissa where they spoke a different language, Oriya. These villagers spoke Hindi and various tribal dialects. Indians generally have a high aptitude for languages and Vijay spoke Hindi fluently. His English was also excellent. I had no difficulty understanding him as he related his story.

His father had turned the family business over to him. It was a large, lucrative shop near the holy city of Puri on the coast of the Bay of Bengal. The famous temple of lord Jaganath, the mysterious black-faced god highly honored by millions, is located there. The annual festival to celebrate this god draws nearly a million pilgrims from across India.

Unfortunately Vijay had made a few bad business decisions, incurring heavy debts. He faced bankruptcy. Vijay found himself under tremendous pressure and self-condemnation. He could not face the shame of losing the prosperous business his father had given him. There was no way out.

Vijay decided to kill himself. (American culture is guilt oriented while India, Sri Lanka, and much of Asia are shame oriented.)

He left his wife and two small children during the night and took a bus to the vicinity of a high bridge where he planned to jump. He thought it was far enough away that no one would be able to recognize his battered body. The burden he carried was unbearable. He wanted to die.

Vijay was from the highest Indian caste, the Brahmins. According to the Hindu religion they were the priestly caste and had the best possibility of escaping the cycle of rebirths upon their death and eventually entering into the blissful state of nirvana. There they would cease to exist as a recognizable individual person or spirit.

Like most Indian men he was accustomed to wearing the traditional Indian kurta, a collarless, long-sleeve shirt that extended below the knees worn over baggy, light, cotton pants. No one was in sight as Vijay climbed up the bridge railing about dawn the next day. He poised himself one rung from the top rail and looked down. Leaning over slightly he closed his eyes preparing to jump when suddenly the back of his shirt was pulled back toward the bridge. Startled he turned to see who had jerked his shirttail. No one was there.

Completely bewildered, Vijay walked across the bridge glancing back every few steps to see who might have pulled at him. It was no hallucination. Someone or something had pulled him from certain death, but no one was in sight.

As a strict Hindu, he had been sheltered from any understanding of Christianity, Jesus, and the possibility of angels. He had no explanation for what had happened. Befuddled, he drudged down the road until suddenly it happened again. This time his shirt was pulled sideways. It pulled him off toward a narrow dirt driveway which he had not noticed. Nestled in the trees at the end of it was a little Christian church.

Vijay looked at me with tender eyes and said, "I heard the Gospel for the first time in that church, and I gave my life to Jesus Christ. He saved me. I have a relationship now with my Heavenly Father."

He grew in his faith and eventually sensed the call of God on his life. After being graduated from a Bible college he joined our dear Brother N. J. Varughese and All India Mission. The church in Daltonganj was planted under this mission and is now the mother church of branch churches in areas where previously there had been no Christian witness.

Vijay obeyed the challenge and command of Jesus. Thousands of faces now reflect the glory of the Lord because of his obedience. Dark, fearful, superstitious eyes have been transformed. The believers of Daltonganj glow with the Spirit of God just as the Apostle Paul exhorted the believers in Rome.

> *Be devoted to one another in brotherly love. Honor one another above yourselves. Never be lacking in zeal, but keep your spiritual fervor, serving the Lord. Be joyful in hope, patient in affliction, faithful in prayer* (Romans 12:10-12 NIV).

Religion is no substitute for a relationship. Vijay had lots of religion. Indian mythology abounds with stories of the gods. That includes Hanuman, half monkey and half man, that jumped from India to Sri Lanka, a distance of 30 miles. Also the god Ganesh, half elephant and half man who is fat and thus personifies wealth and well-being. India today is like the New Testament times. There were many gods then also. Nonetheless, Jesus commanded his disciples to go and preach the Good News and make disciples.

The Apostle Paul declares in the first chapter of Romans that natural revelation – what can be seen in nature and creation itself, plus man being made in the image of God – is enough for man to be without excuse for his wickedness. Instead of drawing near to God human beings became futile in their thinking and their foolish hearts were darkened. Although they claimed to be wise, they became fools and exchanged the glory of the immortal God for images made to look like mortal man and birds and animals and reptiles.

Seven years passed. Vijay's family thought he was dead. He had no communication with them that whole time. Finally he decided to make contact. Two brothers from his team took a taxi to his ancestral home and knocked on the door. They inquired if Vijay lived there but were told that he was dead. The brothers informed the family that Vijay was, indeed, alive and wanted to see them. Eventually Vijay was reunited with his family. His wife and daughter now serve alongside him. His son was graduated from a Bible college and now shares in the ministry with his father.

Stephen and Vijay had their rat in the wall experience in India and then fulfillment in Jesus Christ. I had experienced mine in America. But now Stephen and I were together in Orissa for a few days. Having completed our mission we returned to Calcutta and were reassigned to different teams. Our friendship, however, was established for eternity and our work together on Earth was not finished. There was much more to come.

Chapter
2

TICKLED BY GOD

My journey to India really began five years before the incident at Beniapukur Road. I was a sophomore at the University of Tulsa. Life was good. Life was exciting. My Uncle Max and Aunt Janice had invited me to live with them while I was a student there. Tulsa was almost a thousand miles from my Indiana home and family, but I liked adventure and meeting new people.

After my freshman year Uncle Max received a promotion and was transferred to Chicago. Suddenly I had to find a job so I could afford to live on campus in our fraternity house. A part-time job with Trans World Airlines at the Tulsa International Airport was advertised, and I went for an interview. My uncle had been a supervisor for TWA and fortunately the station manager knew me. I got the job.

As a TWA Transportation Agent, I had a tailor-made airline suit and a shiny, leather-billed hat with the TWA insignia. Most of the time I worked operations for the evening flights. My responsibility was to figure the weight and balance of the aircraft with the proper water and fuel load. Using a long accounting sheet I had to tally up the number of passengers and the luggage breakdown by destination. After it was figured, I typed a ticker tape of the information and sent it to the next airport en route. This was before computers and electronic transfers. It was also my duty to supply the captain with our latest weather reports when he came into the office. Finally, I stood on the tarmac, saluted the pilot after all was clear, and the plane pulled away from the gate.

It was not only an exciting job, but I earned enough working an average of twenty-five hours a week to pay all of my university expenses. Free or discounted tickets were also benefits I really enjoyed, but at the same time I had to discipline myself. I was determined to finish my degree in four years, so my academic load was always full.

Many times I returned to the Pi Kappa Alpha fraternity house after one o'clock in the morning and had to be in class less than seven hours later. Still I was able to make good grades and even made the Dean's List a few times. We also had great parties at 'Pike House' and were successful in the intramural sports program. I was experiencing true independence for the first time in my life and savored every minute of it.

In my sophomore year I studied philosophy and religions. These subjects caused me to think more deeply about life. I found myself questioning things I had apparently taken for granted. Why am I here on earth? Is there any meaning to life? What is after death? Are all religions basically the same? Are there any absolute truths or is all truth relative? Is there something more to life than I am experiencing?

Though Tulsa University had Presbyterian roots, Christianity was not obvious on campus. We were really a secular institution. Dr. Grady Snuggs taught a required New Testament course that intrigued me, but my philosophy professor was an agnostic. A Wesley Foundation Student Center which catered to Methodist students was located near our frat house, but I seldom went there. I didn't attend church much either.

At nineteen and on my own I began to search for meaning. Islam, Hinduism, Buddhism, the Chinese religions, godless philosophies – all had some presence on campus. We had students from many nations, especially the Middle East, who had come to study Petroleum Engineering. The university, located in an oil industry hub, was acclaimed internationally for this academic department.

All the religions and philosophies seemed to mesh into one stream – man's attempt to find a reason for his existence. The conclusion, as I understood it, was basically do your best to do good rather than evil or bad things and in the end you will be all right if your good is weightier than your bad. But this was no answer for the emptiness I was feeling inside.

At that time if someone had asked me if I was a Christian, I would have said, "Yes, I am a Methodist." In my quest for truth, however, I had neglected to seriously investigate the claims of Jesus Christ. Sometimes we overlook that which has become common. A big change was about to take place in my life. Though I had a good life by most worldly standards, there was a consistent thought that often came to my mind, *This is not it!* Nothing seemed to satisfy me on the deepest level. Life for me had temporary highs followed by haunting echoes – *This is not it! This is not it!*

At one of our fraternity business meetings our president announced that a special religious meeting would soon be held in our living room. A representative of Campus Crusade for Christ was scheduled to speak. About twenty brothers gathered that evening to hear Paul Dunham. It was not exactly a religious talk as I anticipated. Instead, he emphasized the person of Jesus Christ and spoke as if Jesus was his personal friend.

My mind began to whirl. *Maybe this was what I was missing. Perhaps I had overlooked Christianity assuming I knew what it was about.* The seeds of faith were planted in me. I used to attend my Uncle Sam and Aunt Mary's church, Main Street Methodist. It was only a few blocks from our home. It had a good basketball team and some really nice looking girls. Dad and Mom went occasionally if they were not working. They made sure that my brother, Steve, and I were baptized there as infants. Later I took the confirmation classes and became a member.

At the university I chose history as my major, and I planned to become a high school or college teacher. I believed that Jesus was a historical figure and that He accomplished a great deal in His short life span. I even confessed Him as my Savior before joining the church back then. I recognized Jesus as an important person, but so were Abraham Lincoln, George Washington, Mohammed, Buddha, and many others in world history.

That night at the fraternity house Paul Dunham, our guest speaker, talked like he had a personal relationship with Jesus. He did not talk about the historical Jesus as much as he emphasized that Jesus was alive today. He did not emphasize that He was a good influence by the example of the godly life He lived. Dunham's point was this: Jesus Christ is alive and still saving souls. He quoted, *What will it profit a man if he gains the whole world, and loses his own soul?* (Mark 8:36). How could I lose my soul? He quoted another verse which I already knew from my Sunday School days, *For God so loved the world that He gave His only begotten Son, that whosoever believes in Him should not perish but have everlasting life* (John 3:16). He caused me to wonder if I had this everlasting life or was I perishing?

The message that night was informative, but I was left with more questions than answers until his closing remarks. He challenged me to trust in Jesus, to put full confidence in Him, to believe that He died for my sins, and that God raised Him up on the third day. At the close of the meeting Paul asked us to bow our heads and pray a simple prayer with him. It went something like this, "God, thank you for sending Jesus to die on the cross for me. I am a sinner for Your Word says that all have sinned and come short of the glory of God. Forgive me. I ask you to come into my life tonight. Your Word says that as many as receive Christ to them He gave power to become the children of God (John 1:12). Thank you for coming into my life tonight."

I don't know how many of the fraternity brothers sincerely prayed that prayer, but I did. There was no immediate sensation that I recall, but Paul pointed out another Scripture. *Therefore, if anyone is in Christ, he is a new creation; the old is gone, the new is come!* (2 Corinthians 5:17 NIV). My commitment to Jesus Christ and receiving Him into my life was an act of faith. It was not *blind faith* but reasoned faith. As the prophet Isaiah said,

> Come now, and let us reason together," says the LORD, "Though your sins are like scarlet, they shall be white as snow; though they are red like crimson, they shall be as wool" (Isaiah 1:18).

This reasoning made sense to me for it seemed more compatible with science. The science disciplines always interested me, especially the physical sciences. I recall sitting with some of the inquisitive brothers on the red fire truck (our Pike symbol) in front of the house at night. We gazed up at the stars and discussed the possibilities of life on other planets. I could never convince myself that everything happened by accident – chance plus time.

One morning I arrived early for my biology class. The Science Building doors were still locked, and several students were standing around at the entrance. I found a shaded spot next to the building and squatted down in the landscaped rock garden. We had been studying genetics for a couple of weeks. I opened my textbook and flipped the pages until I came to the familiar 'XY' chapter. This was months after I had prayed with Paul to receive Jesus Christ into my life. My faith was growing, but I had lots of questions. As I crouched there contemplating the formulas of egg and sperm, gender, fertilization and genetic traits, I honestly questioned, *Where is God in this?*

Something under my right shoe was pressing hard against my foot. I shifted my weight to the left foot and reached to feel for the object. To my utter amazement it was a stone the size of a medium chicken egg, an exact replica of a human fetus with head, eyes, ears, developing extremities including a bud-like tail. The resemblance was exact, beyond imagination. I trembled.

What is the mathematical probability that a quarried stone so perfectly shaped would be in that rock garden outside the Tulsa University Science Building at the very moment I was contemplating my origins? It was there pushing against my foot! Psalm 139:15-16 says that God knew us before we were formed in our mother's womb. When Jesus Christ made His triumphal entry into Jerusalem, the whole multitude of disciples began to rejoice and praise God with a loud voice for all the mighty works they had seen. But the very religious Pharisees called to Jesus from the crowd, "Teacher, rebuke your disciples."

> *But He answered and said to them, "I tell you that if these should keep silent, the stones would immediately cry out"* (Luke 19:40).

It was as if the stone lodged against my foot was crying out to me, "I the Lord am your Creator."

During the months that followed, noticeable changes occurred in me. Fraternity brothers saw me consistently smiling. One brother asked, "What's happened to you?"

Because my Bible knowledge was minimal, I didn't quote Scriptures. I naively said, "God's tickling me on the inside, man." I had no shame about it. That was my feeble attempt to describe what I was feeling.

Today it seems that the pendulum has swung in Christianity to the mental ascent side. The current trend is just a positive confession and accepting information. Believe the right dogma and follow the steps to success. The emotion and reality of true spiritual conversion has been downplayed. Just believe matter of fact. It's a done deal.

Being born is an experience! I don't remember the experience of entering into this world at St. Joseph's Hospital in Kokomo, Indiana, on November 16, 1943, but I am sure it was traumatic. I am sure there were lots of emotions and physical sensations.

Being born again is also an experience! I had asked the Creator of the universe to forgive me. I received his Son into my body which was now His temple. Should I not expect to feel something?

> *Here I am! I stand at the door and knock. If anyone hears my voice and opens the door, I will come in and eat with him, and he with me* (Revelation 3:20 NIV).

That is an experience available to both the church and the individual. The terminology that I did not know then was 'born of God' or literally from the Greek 'born from above.'

> *He was in the world, and though the world was made through him, the world did not recognize him. He came to that which was*

his own, but his own did not receive him. Yet to all who received him, to those who believed in his name, he gave the right to become the children of God — children born not of natural descent, nor of human decision or a husband's will, but born of God (John 1:10-13 NIV).

Jesus spoke to a very religious man when He said,

I tell you the truth, no one can see the kingdom of God unless he is born again (John 3:3 NIV).

I had not simply acquired some new knowledge. Something happened inside my physical body when I repented for my sins. Jesus emphasized the necessity of repenting. *I tell you, no; but unless you repent you will all likewise perish* (Luke 13:5). The Apostle Paul also recognized a godly sorrow that produced repentance leading to salvation in 2 Corinthians 7:10a. Jesus further illustrated this new birth stemming from repentance by setting a child before His disciples and saying,

Assuredly, I say to you, unless you are converted and become as little children, you will by no means enter the kingdom of heaven (Matthew 18:3 NIV).

People are desperately searching for thrills and adventure, something to make them feel good and vibrantly alive. Drugs are rampant because they make you feel so good. Sometimes they make you feel invincible. I have learned that they are counterfeits, substitutes for the Truth. The Greek word for spirits is *pharmakeia* from which we derive 'pharmacy' and is related to witchcraft. The prophet Samuel spoke to the wayward King Saul, *For rebellion is like the sin of witchcraft and stubbornness is as iniquity and idolatry* (I Samuel 15:23 NIV). The drug culture of today is nothing but rebellion towards God. Those who get caught up in it are exposing themselves to real evil spirits.

I met a missionary to the Arabs who had been an honor student at Harvard University but dropped out to join a commune in Arizona. He became enthralled with American Indian culture and soon was smoking a hallucinogenic cactus. His sister was a Christian believer and had given him a New Testament. She prayed that God would save him. Eventually a bad trip convinced him that evil was definitely real. He opened himself up to the spirit world and was frightened beyond words. Coming to his right mind, he began to study the New Testament thoroughly and accepted Christ.

Much is being trumpeted today about being high on this or that. Some say, "stoned out of your mind." Basically they are talking about a feeling, a physical sensation. We are creatures of feeling. If there is a God, He should be able to affect us in that part of our being. Was this the tickling I was experiencing? Indeed, it was more than a physical sensation. I felt light in heart. It seemed that the grass was greener. The birds were singing just for me. Indescribable peace filled my mind. A still small voice within said, "This is it!" I felt whole as a person. My spirit became alive.

At the same time I began to hunger for knowledge. My understanding of the Word had to catch up to my experience. The Gideon New Testament on my desk which I neglected before was suddenly understandable. I could not get enough of the Word. It was like a treasure chest filled with gems of practical insight into life.

I concentrated at first on the Book of John.

In the beginning was the Word, and the Word was with God, and the Word was God. He was with God in the beginning. Through him all things were made; without him nothing was made that has been made. In him was life, and that life was the light of men. The light shines in the darkness, but the darkness has not understood it (John 1:1-5). *The Word became flesh and made his dwelling among us. We have seen his glory, the glory of the One and Only, who came from the Father, full of grace and truth* (John 1:14 NIV).

The Word of God and Jesus Christ were now central to my very being. I had peace with my Heavenly Father.

But Stephen in India knew nothing of Jesus, the Bible, or even that a Christian Church existed. Yet when he called on the name of the Lord, he experienced something very wonderful. I knew about Jesus, the Bible, and attended church occasionally but was lacking an experience. Why? A great Methodist missionary once made a very pertinent remark along these lines. He said that we in Christianized countries have been inoculated with a weak form of Christianity which often makes us immune to the real thing. That made sense to me.

I understood the scientific corollary. For example, we are infected with a slight case of smallpox when we are pricked with the vaccine. This prevents us from getting a full-fledged case of this horrible, disfiguring disease. I was injected now with the real thing.

For you did not receive the spirit of bondage again to fear, but you received the Spirit of adoption by whom we cry out, "Abba Father." The Spirit Himself bears witness with our spirit that we are children of God (Romans 8:15-16).

29

As my knowledge began to catch up to my experience, my spiritual appetite increased exponentially. I loved learning more than ever. I became a voracious reader. History, science, philosophy – almost every subject interested me. My quest for knowledge was not limited to the Christian perspective. I read books by agnostics, atheists, existentialists, and of other religions. I wanted to know what they believed. Why did they not believe in the historical God of the Bible and in Jesus Christ?

Christians are criticized for being narrow-minded, accused of being ostriches with their heads stuck in a hole in the sand, oblivious to the real world. This was not the case with me nor with the many Christians I began to know and read about in history. It was a very bad generalization. I discovered that there were many renowned scientists, social reformers, humanitarians, artists, thinkers, and writers who were Christians.

Many of our Asian friends today are from non-Christian backgrounds. After becoming believers they also hungered for more knowledge. Pastor Susiri in Colombo, Sri Lanka, has become a very close family friend. He was once a staunch Buddhist and attempted to disrupt a public meeting where a Christian evangelist was speaking. Before he could do his dirty work the message struck a responsive chord in his heart. He responded to the invitation to receive the Lord Jesus Christ and was later graduated from college. He told me that the lightness of heart which he felt at that first meeting with Christ has stayed with him to this day, thirty-five years later. He has been a pastor for more than thirty years now presenting the Gospel effectively to the Buddhists since he is so well acquainted with their philosophy.

Iqubal Q. was a young teenager from a Muslim family in north India. When he heard the Gospel preached by one of our OM teams, he believed and experienced this new birth. Now he has two earned doctorates and has a ministry to bring the Christian message to his Muslim friends.

The decade of the sixties was filled with turmoil – hippies and drugs, war protests and violent campus demonstrations, and free sex. There was also a Jesus Movement. Campus Crusade for Christ was an important part of that Christian renewal on university campuses throughout the world. One of those faithful campus ministers was Paul Dunham. His coming to Tulsa University and our fraternity changed the course of my life. He later became Dr. Dunham and is now a retired university professor. He and his dear wife, Sandy, remain close friends.

The founder of the Methodist Church was John Wesley from

England. He was raised in a very religious home. He even studied for the ministry and became a missionary to the American Indians in Georgia. There he failed miserably and returned to his homeland in defeat. He felt like he himself had a need to be converted. John Wesley was highly educated at Oxford University but truly empty inside. In a meeting, which he reluctantly attended, the minister was reading Luther's preface to the Book of Romans when Wesley felt his heart strangely warmed. From then on he became a dynamic preacher wherever he could share the Good News – even in open-air meetings which was unheard of in his Anglican tradition.

Being tickled by God opened my spiritual eyes.

I pray also that the eyes of your heart may be enlightened in order that you may know the hope to which he has called you, the riches of his glorious inheritance in the saints (Ephesians 1:18 NIV).

I began loving God which was a new experience for me. When you love someone, you want to hang out with that person. You are attentive to what they have to say. How can you love something or someone you cannot see?

When I received Jesus Christ – when I believed and trusted solely in him for the forgiveness of my sins not relying on any good works of my own – God gave me new birth (John 1:12-13). The central evidence confirming the authenticity of my experience – Bible evidence – was what I now call 'the love factor.' *No one has ever seen God; but if we love one another, God lives in us and his love is made complete in us* (1 John 4:12 NIV). The religious Pharisees tested Jesus with a question as to which is the greatest commandment in the law. Jesus replied,

'Love the Lord your God with all your heart and with all your soul and with all your mind.' This is the first and greatest commandment. And the second is like it, 'Love your neighbor as yourself.' All the Law and the Prophets hang on these two commandments (Matthew 22:37-40 NIV).

I now loved God and my Indian brothers and sisters. My family love circle was growing from Indiana to India. I saw evidence of God's love in my teammates as well. Hindus and Muslims often have violent clashes in India. The hatred goes back to the partition days when colonial India was divided into Hindu India and Muslim East and West Pakistan During that period countless thousands were killed in bloody rioting. You can understand the tension. The Muslims love beef shish kebob roasted over glowing coals. The Hindus worship the cow. That is ample cause for rioting in itself. But on our Gospel team I saw brothers loving each other despite such opposite backgrounds. We were really one in the Lord.

Years later in Sri Lanka I saw two ethnic groups at war – the Tamils who are mostly Hindus, and the Singhalese who are predominately Buddhists. Christians from both communities loved each other in the Lord.

> We love because he first loved us. If anyone says, 'I love God,' yet hates his brother, he is a liar. For anyone who does not love his brother, whom he has seen, cannot love God, whom he has not seen. And he has given us this command: Whoever loves God must also love his brother (1 John 4:19-21 NIV).

God gave me a love for the people of India. I did not have this before He tickled me. Nor did I have a desire to go around the world to share the love of God with them. As I studied the Scriptures, my heart was expanded. The Word of God explained what I was feeling.

> For Christ's love compels us, because we are convinced that one died for all, and therefore all died. And he died for all, that those who live should no longer live for themselves but for him who died for them and was raised again. So from now on we regard no one from a worldly point if view. Though we once regarded Christ in this way, we do so no longer (2 Corinthians 5:14-16 NIV).

People everywhere took on new significance in my thinking. Everyone was important in God's sight. I began caring for others like I had not cared before. Certainly this was an extreme adventure for me. I felt that God was working in my heart and that He was guiding me to help others find the Truth.

Over the years now I have met thousands of brothers and sisters in Christ who have a definite conversion experience. Their stories are all unique and would make an appropriate sequel to this book. Let me tell you a recent one. I met Paul on the Dutch island of Aruba in September, 2005. He was our taxi driver in Oranjestad. We shared our testimony with him as he drove us to a nice seafood restaurant.

Before we arrived at our destination he said, "Now let me tell you my story. I was a fisherman and had my own boat. My lifestyle had no place for God. I was far from Him. Over the years I did not realize that the long pants I wore would be my demise. They were continually wet from fishing in the sea. The doctors surmised that some kind of sea poisoning was absorbed into my lower extremities from my damp trousers. Gradually I became paralyzed from the waist down and was hospitalized for eighteen months.

"Someone told their pastor to visit me in the hospital. He came and gave me a Bible. I started to read it. After a month or so I really cried out to God. 'Lord, I need you to come into my life. Please do something in me.' Nothing happened. Days later, I continued reading and again cried out in desperation. 'Lord, God, do something in me. I need to know you.' Suddenly I felt an awesome power enter my body under the left armpit. The power surged up and down my frame and then left me.

"I scooted over to the edge of the bed and maneuvered my legs off the mattress. They dangled lifelessly above the floor, but inspired by God's touch I lifted myself and stood up for the first time in a year and a half. Then I took my first steps. I could walk again. From then on the Bible became the source of my life. I drive this taxi, but I have also shared my testimony in the United States and other countries. God has led me to accept invitations and opened doors that I never imagined."

That statement agrees with my experience as well. He not only saves us, but He leads us too. He has a plan for our lives. The Twenty-third Psalm that is so often quoted for comfort when facing death is just as appropriate in facing life.

> *The Lord is my shepherd; I shall not want. He makes me to lie down in green pastures; he leads me beside the still waters. He restores my soul; he leads me in the paths of righteousness for His name's sake* (Psalm 23:1-3). Jesus said, *The thief does not come except to steal, and to kill, and to destroy. I have come that they may have life, and that they may have it more abundantly* (John 10:10).

The New Testament experience of Christianity is that God truly leads His people. They each have a unique destiny. He has a plan for every life. I was tickled for a purpose. My next step was about to be revealed.

Chapter
3

Asbury Assignment

I was a cadet in the US Air Force ROTC unit at Tulsa University. Military life seemed to agree with me. The discipline, order, and promise of adventure were appealing. In my junior year I was assigned to summer camp at Lockbourne Air Force Base near Columbus, Ohio. Morning reveille blared through the barracks at 4:30 am. We had only 30 minutes to prepare for inspection. I learned to spit shine my boots the night before in order to save precious time in the morning. The sergeant's piercing glare did not miss a thing out of order.

I also learned that I needed to listen well and carry out the exact command or I would suffer the consequences. One morning we were marching in platoon formation before sunrise, and I was the lead man in our file. Unfortunately I did not hear the command, "To the rear, march!" Consequently I continued to march straight ahead until I realized that I was marching alone. The platoon marched off in the opposite direction! I don't know if I had a mental lapse or was day-dreaming, but it was an embarrassing moment. I quickly turned, ran back to the platoon, and shuffle-stepped to the cadence of my file until I was back in formation. We can also certainly miss much more important things in life if we are not attentive.

After being tickled by God and increasingly captivated by His Word, I desired to know His will for my life. I realized that I was not a creature of chance or of man's will alone. I believe John 1:12-13 which says,

> Yet to all who received him, to those who believed in his name, he gave the right to become children of God — children born not of natural descent, nor of human decision or a husband's will, but born of God (NIV).

He had a destiny for me. Even science confirmed what I was

thinking. Each human being is unique with a one-of-a-kind fingerprint and DNA.

Contrarily, the bottom line of the evolution theory, as I understood it, was that time and chance gave birth to humanity. That required a lot of blind faith, especially as I learned the complex symmetrical design of the DNA molecule. That design has a code. In other words it has a language. It is not chaotic. That fact agreed with the Word of God which says that God spoke creation into existence. His language is the code behind creation – not a chance or random cosmic explosion. Genesis, the first book of the Bible, records, *God said, 'Let there be . . . and it was . . .* (Genesis 1:3). *By faith we understand that the universe was formed at God's command, so that what is seen was not made out of what was visible* (Hebrews 11:3 NIV). The Bible even says that God has the very hairs of your head numbered (Luke 12:7), and all those who belong to Jesus have their name written down in the Book of Life (Revelation 13:8).

I was following my chosen path which was to be a history teacher and also a career Air Force officer. I even signed a contract with the United States Air Force and received a monthly check from the government. At the same time there was a struggle going on inside me. An impression came to my mind that I should preach and teach 'His Story' rather than U.S. or World History. *But couldn't I also serve in the Air Force?* I wondered. One night I returned to the fraternity from my job at the airport and could not sleep. About one in the morning I reached for my Bible and cried out, "Lord, if you want me in the ministry teaching your Word, then show me tonight. I need a confirmation."

I opened the Bible randomly and stuck my finger on a verse.

"Whoever calls on the name of the Lord shall be saved." How then shall they call on Him in whom they have not believed? And how shall they believe in Him of whom they have not heard? And how shall they hear without a preacher? And how shall they preach unless they are sent? (Romans 10:13-15a).

It was the first time I read that in the Bible. Certainly it was an immediate confirmation. In fact that passage of Scripture has been the frame from which my life and ministry has developed for over 40 years – preparing preachers and helping send them to preach the Gospel to those who have not heard the message.

I began to devise a plan that would allow me to stay in the Air Force and serve the Lord at the same time. I would be a chaplain. *That's a great idea,* I thought. It seemed to be the logical choice. There was one big problem – I didn't ask God. I told Him what I would do.

Another night when I could not fall asleep, I paid a visit to a member of our Campus Crusade for Christ staff. She lived a few blocks away from the Pike House. Ann made a statement that night which caused me to change my plans. "Whatever you do," she said, "do not compromise God's will for your life."

I didn't want to give up my plans for an Air Force career. I envisioned myself driving a dark green sports car through the Pyrenees of southwestern Europe while dressed in my Air Force uniform with shiny lieutenant bars on my shoulders. I thought it would be an admirable career. I met several chaplains and liked what they said about serving in the military. Merlin Carothers, who wrote *Prison to Praise*, had a great ministry as a chaplain. His book became very popular during that decade, touching thousands with the message of "praising God in all circumstances." I met him in the early 70's at the Annual Conference of the United Methodist Church in Lafayette, Indiana. I was also ordained as a Methodist minister in that same conference.

For me, the old adage applied, "The good is often the enemy of the better, and the better is the enemy of the best." There was no peace in my heart for the chaplaincy, and I knew God wanted me to be at peace.

> *Let the peace of Christ rule in your hearts, since as members of*
> *one body you were called to peace* (Colossians 3:15 NIV).

I needed to be willing to give up that aspiration. With that surrender came peace but also uncertainty. What was I to do now? A military career had been my dream for years.

One thing was evident in my pattern of thinking since praying the sinner's prayer with Paul Dunham. There was a knowing, an assurance that God had a plan – an assignment – for my life.

> *I write these things to you who believe in the name of the Son of*
> *God so that you may know that you have eternal life* (1 John 5:13
> NIV).

No amount of money, riches, fame, or anything the world has to offer is comparable to the assurance of that knowing.

The second week of our AF ROTC summer camp included survival training. We were blindfolded and herded into troop transports. They attempted to further disorient us by driving around for several miles, making numerous turns and reversals. Finally we came to an abrupt halt. The sergeant unlatched the two side hitches and yelled for us to jump out. Removing our blindfolds we found ourselves at the bottom of a gravel pit.

We were given the co-ordinates of home base where there was supposed to be drinking water and food. We had none with us. Only a compass, a terrain map, and two flashlights were issued to us as the truck pulled away. The sun was setting. Darkness was soon upon us.

Among the cadets we had some future pilots and navigators who knew how to read a terrain map. They surveyed the surrounding environment, laid the map on the ground, and positioned the compass on the map. One of the navigators handed me a flashlight and told me to start walking up toward the woods above the quarry walls.

I walked until he yelled for me to stop. He then gave me instructions to move several steps to my right as I directed the light toward the platoon. When I got in the right place according to the reading of the compass on the map, he yelled for me to stand still until they all came to me, guided by my light. It was now pitch dark, and I was their guiding light.

I stood there probably fifty yards away until they all made it to my spot at the edge of the forest. Then I went another fifty yards or so until they stopped me again. We repeated the procedure into the early morning hours. We climbed up ravines and clambered over brush piles. Sometimes the forest was so dense I could only go a short distance before they would stop me again.

Finally we made it to the base camp, but there was no water or food. We were supposed to survive on what could be found in the dense woods. In retrospect I realize it was a good experience. Sometime later I saw an analogy with the survival training and my new life in Christ. God has provided all we need to accomplish our assignment here on Earth. The terrain map I imagined was the Bible. It was full of history, geography, poetry, insight, and practical spiritual knowledge. The compass I likened to the Holy Spirit residing in the believer. Jesus had told his followers that he would not leave them as orphans.

> *If you love me, you will obey what I command. And I will ask the Father, and he will give you another Counselor to be with you forever — the Spirit of truth. The world cannot accept him, because it neither sees him nor knows him. But you know him, for he lives with you and will be in you. I will not leave you as orphans; I will come to you* (John 14:15-18 NIV).

This was not an impersonal force or an it. The Holy Spirit you read about in the *Acts of the Apostles* is the very presence of the Lord. Acts 16:7 indicates that the Spirit of Jesus was leading them. Jesus had told them not to leave Jerusalem until the gift promised by the Father had come upon them (Acts 1:4). Following that compass, God's Spirit within you, will always lead to Christ-likeness and God's love.

The flashlight I envisioned as Jesus Christ Himself who said in John 9:5 *"While I am in the world I am the light of the world."* The words of Jesus enthralled me and still do. I came to realize that God is not out there somewhere or simply an idea in my mind. He is the historical God of the Jews whom the Apostle Paul declared to the philosophers of Athens.

> *The God who made the world and everything in it is the Lord of heaven and earth and does not live in temples built by hands. And he is not served by human hands, as if he needed anything, because he himself gives all men life and breath and everything else. From one man he made every nation of men, that they should inhabit the whole earth; and he determined the times set for them and the exact places where they should live. God did this so that men would seek him and perhaps reach out for him and find him, though he is not far from each one of us. For in him we live and move and have our being* (Acts 17:24-26a NIV).

I found that the closer I got to Jesus the closer I felt to God and vice versa.

The summer camp ended. As much as I liked the thought of a military career, I knew God had another assignment for me. I did not have to look far and wide. He sets us in the exact place he wants us. I found myself at the right place at the right time. A tall, slender man sat next to me in psychology class reading his Bible. He said he was a Free Methodist minister and graduate of Asbury Theological Seminary. A Tulsa oilman and philanthropist had granted him a scholarship to go there. The more I learned about Asbury, the greater the conviction that this was God's next assignment for me. There was, however, a looming obstacle in my path.

The Vietnam War was escalating. After resigning from the Air Force ROTC program, the local draft board in Kokomo classified me as 1A. That meant my number could be selected, and I would be in the army instead of preparing for the ministry at Asbury. The Air Force major on campus suggested that I write the draft board asking for an appointment to explain why I had resigned my commission and my present situation. I figured that God would make a way. They understood and granted me a deferment to attend seminary. *The one who calls you is faithful and he will do it* (1 Thessalonians 5:24 NIV).

Asbury Theological Seminary is located in Wilmore, Kentucky, a very small town about a one hour drive from Lexington. The spiritual atmosphere was inspiring. Imagine three hundred hardy men singing, "Amazing love how can it be, that thou my God should die for me." I spent many nights praying in Estes Chapel and the small prayer chapel next to it. One of the true strengths of Asbury was that students were encouraged to develop their prayer and devotional lives. Biblical scholars from various theological persuasions instructed us, though the Methodist tradition was prevalent on campus.

My missions professor was Dr. J. T. Seamands, a second-generation missionary to India. The Indian church affectionately called his father *Tata* Seamands. That was a name of great love and respect in his beloved India meaning Grandfather. *Tata* Seamands had been an engineer by profession and his call to India was extremely dramatic. With his eyes wide open he saw the word 'India' written in flames while kneeling at a church altar call. Through many decades of service in India hundreds of churches were constructed because of his expertise and boundless energy. In his nineties from his hospital bed in India he talked about building just one more church but was encouraged by his son, Dr. David Seamands, to let someone else do it. "Dad, you have done your part. Now just rest and know the Lord is here and ready to receive you into heaven." *Tata* soon thereafter rested from his labors.

Dr. J. T. Seamands was a good friend of the famous evangelist and author, Dr. E. Stanley Jones. They were the core of the Christian ashram movement in India which Dr. Jones initiated. It was a forum and community to reach seekers of truth by emphasizing the uniqueness of the Lord Jesus Christ. True Christian community was practiced with everyone taking their turn from washing dishes to cleaning the toilets.

This was revolutionary in India where the caste system held every one in their place for life. The Brahmins, the priestly caste, were the closest to the gods. You could distinguish what caste individuals were from by their name and background. The Brahmin men wore a rope-like thread over their shoulder. India's one billion people were relegated to one of five major castes. The Untouchables – street sweepers and toilet cleaners – were below that. The Brahmins would avoid any direct contact with them in fear of becoming contaminated. Years later, a Brahmin man purchased a Gospel packet from me in Bihar. Instead of handing me the coins, he tossed them to me. I was considered unclean or an Untouchable by him.

Asbury was my initial and indirect exposure to the Indian

subcontinent. I was intrigued by what I was learning.

Dr. E. Stanley Jones came to Asbury while I was a student there. He was the most erudite and distinctively powerful speaker I had ever heard. His words were enunciated so eloquently and his vocabulary was so awesome and precise that we were all spellbound from the moment he began to speak.

This was the highlight of my Asbury assignment. After one chapel service a group of us students met with Dr. Jones in the cafeteria. I purchased two of his books, *The Word Become Flesh* and *The Sermon On the Mount* which he graciously autographed and penned his famous motto, "Jesus Is Lord," beside his name. He often declared this simple New Testament creed in his meetings while raising his hand and three fingers. Years later I gave this signed copy of *The Word Become Flesh* to my dear Indian brother, Stephen, which he regards as one of his most precious possessions.

Each evening Estes Chapel was alive with anticipation of Dr. Jones speaking in those special services. At the time he was in his mid 80's with neatly cropped pure white hair on his perfectly erect frame. Though he was less than six feet tall, his very presence in the pulpit was striking. His countenance glowed with the Holy Spirit's power.

He spoke about his life experiences and how the Holy Scriptures reveal the central theme of the Kingdom of God. Later I discovered that what he shared in those chapel services was incorporated into his autobiography, *The Song of Ascents*, which was not yet published but which I later read with great interest.

He emphasized in that message his 'listening post.' "In fifty-two years of ministry," he declared, "I set aside a time in which I quiet my heart and mind before the Lord. I simply listen. In those fifty-two years I have only missed His voice twice. Those two times I undoubtedly followed the voice of my subconscious which became obvious after some time. Do you need specific guidance? You need to establish a *listening post*. Our Father wants to speak to you personally." What Dr. Jones said lined up with Scripture since Jesus, Himself, said that His sheep know His voice (John 10:4).

The Bible tells us that the prophet Elijah hid in a cave because he was afraid. He complained that he had been zealous for the Lord God Almighty but now felt abandoned and alone. 1 Kings 19:11-13 relates what happened. God caused a powerful wind to rip the mountain apart, but the Lord was not in the wind. Then there was an earthquake, but the

Lord was not in the earthquake. Next came a fire, but the Lord was not in the fire. Finally a gentle whisper – a still small voice – and Elijah knew God had spoken.

Dr. Jones made his point. God speaks to the deepest part of your being – your spirit. When God tickled me inside, it was my spirit coming to life. The Bible says that I was dead in my sins but made alive in Christ by His Spirit. Ephesians chapter two clarifies this fact.

There was a long pause. Dr. Jones lowered his voice and whispered, "Tonight God wants to speak to you. Will you listen?" Utter silence swept over the chapel. I closed my eyes and waited. Suddenly still with my eyes closed I saw letters coming from the left on the screen of my mind. It was like reading the message of an electronic signboard, "FEED . . . MY . . . SHEEP."

My heart began to flutter. Excitement welled up within me. *That's really scriptural*, I thought. Anticipating more, I questioned the Lord. *Where, Lord? I am ready to go now. I'll leave seminary and go wherever you want me to go. Where do you want me to feed your sheep?* The silence was deafening but shining letters began to slowly emerge from the left again. I read them in my mind as my eyes remained tightly closed, "WHERE...YOU...ARE." My knees began to shake. I knelt at the pew. God had spoken to me not in an audible voice but in lights.

It was not what I had expected, but I began to do in seminary what He had commanded. I began to minister God's word to my fellow seminarians — in small informal groups, in the dormitory, and in the classroom, God gave me an assignment at Asbury in Wilmore, Kentucky. Ministry opportunities also opened at the area veteran's hospital and at a juvenile detention center.

Dr. Robert Coleman was our professor of evangelism. His book, *The Master Plan of Evangelism*, examined the method of Jesus in training His disciples to reach the world with the Good News. One of the principles was simply that Jesus was "with" them. He truly poured himself into his disciples. Dr. Coleman did the same with a select group of students. We would meet in his office at six in the morning for prayer. I can still see his glowing face looking up as he knelt by his swivel chair, broad angelic smile, and then spontaneous heavenly laughter. It was contagious and quite evident that he really enjoyed his relationship with God.

He was a Ph.D. and practiced what he taught. Regularly we would preach on the streets of Lexington. Dr. Coleman, grinning from ear to ear, boldly preached the Gospel to all who passed by or took the time to stand and listen. We distributed tracts and counseled any who asked for help. You could call it Dr. Coleman's mobile classroom. God had sovereignly planned all these experiences for my Asbury assignment, and they were to greatly influence my future ministry.

Asbury Theological Seminary was named in honor of Francis Asbury, one of the early circuit-riding preachers whom John Wesley sent to the New World. He later became a Methodist bishop and endeavored to preach the Gospel wherever he could find people who might listen. His evangelistic fervor never wavered. Rev. Frank Morris, one of the early presidents of the seminary, was also a fiery evangelistic preacher and a man of great integrity. I was privileged to meet his wife and pray with her at the Warren Methodist Home in Warren, Indiana. She was affectionately known as The Prayer Lady and was often called upon to intercede for others though she was 102 years old at that time. Evangelistic passion, practical holiness, and an emphasis on personal devotion to the Lord and the Word were the wonderful heritage of Asbury which impacted my life.

Ecclesiastes chapter three and verse one says, *To everything there is a season, a time for every purpose under heaven.* Romans 12:1 (NIV) says, *Therefore, I urge you, brothers, in view of God's mercies, to offer your bodies as living sacrifices, holy and pleasing to God — this is your spiritual act of worship.* I had stepped out in faith to attend this institution of higher learning sincerely believing that this was God's will for my life. Yes, there were sacrifices to be made. There was a risk that I might be drafted into the Army. There was a risk that the money would not be there to pay all the bills since the scholarship was only a partial one. There were no full scholarships offered. No one in my family had walked this way before me. I was pioneering virgin territory, but I had an assurance that God was with me leading my steps. He was not only my Savior now, but the Creator God had become my friend as well.

This was an amazing thought, but it was not unheard of. Both the Muslims and the Jews regard Abraham as the father of their faith. He was a very wealthy sheepherder who left all that was familiar to him in obedience to God's command.

> *Now the Lord had said to Abram: 'Get out of your country, from your family and from your father's house, to a land that I will show you. I will make you a great nation; I will bless you and*

> *make your name great; and you shall be a blessing. I will bless those who bless you, and I will curse him who curses you; and in you all the families of the earth shall be blessed* (Genesis 12:1-3).

In the New Testament we read,

> *And the Scripture was fulfilled which says, 'Abraham believed God, and it was accounted to him for righteousness.' And he was called the friend of God* (James 2:23).

Jesus also said,

> *No longer do I call you servants, for a servant does not know what his master is doing; but I have called you friends, for all things that I heard from My Father I have made known to you* (John 15:15).

I recognized early in my relationship with God that I no longer belonged to myself. The physical body I lived in was a temporary dwelling. It was not mine but was now the temple of the Living God.

> *Or do you not know that your body is the temple of the Holy Spirit who is in you, whom you have from God, and that you are not your own? For you have been bought at a price: therefore glorify God in your body* (1 Corinthians 6:19-20a).

This was revolutionary thinking. I belonged to God as one of his called out ones which is what the Greek word *ecclesia* means and is translated in the English Bibles as 'church.' This is true New Testament Christianity.

The Apostle Paul gave his farewell greeting to the church in Ephesus with these pertinent words,

> *I consider my life worth nothing to me, if only I may finish the race and complete the task the Lord Jesus has given me — the task of testifying to the gospel of God's grace* (Acts 20:24 NIV). *Therefore take heed to yourselves and to all the flock, among which the Holy Spirit has made you overseers, to shepherd the church of God which He purchased with His own blood* (Acts 20:28).

What is of supreme importance in those verses? God's love through the sacrifice of His Son Jesus Christ is number one. Number two is the fact that Paul exemplified the truth that we are not our own and that God calls us to care for others.

My time at Asbury was for a season. God had an interruption in the plan, but it was all part of His master blueprint. I had much to learn. One of my seminary professors wrote a book about the psychology of conversion. The intent was to explain in modern psychological terms what actually occurs when a person is born from above. The professors in seminary had Ph.D.'s. Greek and Hebrew scholars, men and women who had given their lives for the truth of the Bible message, surrounded me.

I later discovered the books of Dr. Francis Schaeffer. *The God Who Is There* and *How Shall We Then Live* helped me grasp the truth and development of the faith in the historical context. Dr. Schaeffer convinced many atheists and agnostics that Christianity was true. He and his wife, Edith, established a fellowship in Switzerland to help enquiring people discover the reality of a personal relationship with God. I attended one of his seminars in Indianapolis and talked with him personally.

I read Josh McDowell's book, *Evidence That Demands a Verdict*, and *Honest to God* by J. B. Philips. John R. Stott's books were also helpful. In understanding the nature of man and God's working in him, a Chinese Christian, Watchman Nee, answered many of my questions. In his three-volume classic, *The Spiritual Man*, Nee clarifies the distinction of man's body, soul, and spirit.

Of course the main book of study in seminary was the Bible itself. I believed the Bible was the Word of God for many reasons. I compared it to all the other holy books and religious writings. Only the Bible had, as one author titled his book, *The Ring of Truth*. In other words the historical flow and practical insight of the Scriptures speaks for the veracity of the miraculous. The only plausible cause for the existence of the church is the resurrection from the dead of the Lord Jesus Christ as recorded in the Word.

I found in the very first verse of the Bible all we know that exists in the universe. *In the beginning God created the heavens and the earth (Genesis 1:1).* 'In the beginning' reveals the element of time. 'God' reveals the element of order or intelligent design. 'Created' reveals the element of energy. 'The heavens' reveal the element of space and 'the earth' exemplifies the element of matter. This was not a coincidence.

One former agnostic was asked why he believed the Bible was true and the very Word of God. He answered with just one word, "Israel." The Bible is up-to-date. The prophecies that pertain to the country of Israel, which became a recognized nation again in 1948, are phenomenal. My father and I visited Jerusalem in 1966. At that time the city was controlled by Gentiles (non Jews). A year later Israel took Jerusalem in a lightning war and holds it until this day. I believe this is in fulfillment of Luke 21:24 where Jesus says,

And they will fall by the edge of the sword, and be led away captive into all nations. And Jerusalem will be trampled by Gentiles until the times of the Gentiles are fulfilled.

The prophecies that related to the coming of the Messiah were also very convincing. More than 700 years before Jesus Christ appeared, Isaiah 53 clearly spoke of the suffering and subsequent victory of the Messiah. Jesus Christ was evident in this passage but also in hundreds of other passages. This was not by chance. Jesus Himself viewed the Scriptures as the Word of God. He said in His Sermon on the Mount,

For assuredly, I say to you, till heaven and earth pass away, one jot or tittle will by no means pass from the law till all is fulfilled (Matthew 5:18).

Jesus also understood the significance of His words which is clear from John 6:63, *It is the Spirit who gives life; the flesh profits nothing. The words that I speak to you are spirit, and they are life.*

Surrounded by scholars and books I found my heart still yearning for something more. There was a cry for reality from deep within me. I wanted to experience more of what the Bible was talking about. Jesus said,

But you, when you pray, go into your room, and when you have shut your door, pray to your Father who is in the secret place; and your Father who sees in secret will reward you openly (Matthew 6:6).

I cloistered myself in the little closet of our dormitory room located above the administration offices at Asbury Seminary. I remember the coat hangers tinkling as I desperately flailed my arms beseeching the Lord to show me spiritual reality.

I wanted to experience what New Testament believers experienced. Martyrdom? Well, at least I had to know that I was willing to die for Jesus and for the sake of the Gospel. The Lord had given some incredible challenges to those who would be his disciples.

If anyone would come after me, he must deny himself and take up his cross daily and follow me. For whoever wants to save his life will lose it, but whoever loses his life for me will save it (Luke 9:23-24 NIV).

Was I ready to lose my life for Jesus Christ? Jim Elliott, along with his fellow missionaries in South America, had lost his life for Jesus while trying to make contact with a tribe in the dense rain forest. Long before he was killed by the Auca warriors he had written in his diary, "He is no fool who gives what he cannot keep to gain what he can not lose." That simple but profound statement had stuck in my mind for years.

When my roommate came in, he must have thought that I had gone off the deep end. The noise behind the closet door was, however, my clamoring for reality. I poured out my heart in earnest prayer and slumped in exhaustion. There was nothing more to do than be quiet and wait, but almost immediately I heard an answer so definite I still do not know if it was audible or just a thought, "Go to India."

I was surprised. It was not what I had expected. I knew for a fact that India was a country of great idolatry. They worshipped literally millions of gods. Even the snake, the monkey, and rats were worshipped. The seed of that word grew in my heart. It was nourished by many confirmations. Over the next several months that command became a conviction. I would find spiritual reality in India.

I met a classmate who had worked among the Muslims in Turkey for a year. He was planning to return with the same organization after finishing seminary. It was an international training movement called Operation Mobilization. We met regularly for prayer and Scripture memorization. Could OM India be the interruption in my seminary studies that God had planned for me?

The financial policy for everyone joining an OM team was that you could raise half of your support by selling your possessions and half through prayer. You could let people know what you were going to do, but you were encouraged not to ask directly for financial help. George Mueller of England was used as an example. He founded orphanages and never directly solicited funds. The Lord always met their needs and his work flourished.

I sold my car and a couple of hunting rifles and began to send regular prayer letters to friends who said they would like to hear from me. The circle of friends began to grow as I shared in churches and Christian home cells. I spoke about the Lord's command to *go and make disciples of all nations* (Matthew 28:19 NIV) and then shared my call to India. After the service those interested in receiving my newsletters would stop by a table where I had a sign-up sheet. Some of those people who committed themselves to pray in 1968 are still prayer partners 38 years later. Others have gone as missionaries themselves.

Discipleship was stressed in OM teachings and conferences. We were required to read many challenging books like *Calvary Road* by Roy Hession and *True Discipleship* by William McDonald. The main emphasis was world evangelization through international teams using Christian literature. I went on a Christmas crusade to Mexico and realized that OM was like being in the military. I liked it. Mexico was a good introduction for my future ministry in India.

Chapter
4

ABUNDANT LIFE?

George Verwer, the International Coordinator and co-founder of Operation Mobilization, was the keynote speaker for the new American summer recruits. His impassioned challenges for true discipleship set the tone for our week of teaching and training in London and stirred us to abandon ourselves to the Lord.

The conference in 1968 was blessed also to have as one of its speakers Rev. Richard Wurmbrand who had been recently released from a terrible communist prison in Romania. His crime? As a Lutheran pastor he refused to compromise his Christian message. His whole family paid a horrible price, but now he was free to tell the world. His book, *Tortured for Christ*, made me cringe and weep. At the conference he removed his shirt to reveal holes and scars that red-hot branding irons had seared into his flesh. It was difficult to imagine that a man could endure such torture with its excruciating physical and mental pain. Rev. Wurmbrand not only endured. He came forth victoriously! God used him and his wife to minister effectively to the families of martyrs and imprisoned Christians behind the iron curtain. My heart was challenged. I am thankful that God brought such dedicated men and women across my path.

The OM emphasis was world evangelism through international teams mainly using Christian literature. I had participated with OM in a Christmas crusade in Mexico, but this was my first European experience.

Seasoned OM-trained people usually led the teams, but that summer there was a shortage of veterans. Greg Livingstone, (one of the international leaders who later went on to establish Frontiers, a ministry uniquely called to reach Muslims), knew me and recommended that I lead the team to Caspe, Spain, in the Zaragoza district west of Barcelona. It is my firm conviction that when you abandon yourself to the Lord Jesus, determined to obey his challenge and command, the Father brings people into your life to help you accomplish your destiny.

Greg Livingstone and I had met in Florida when he was there to officiate at the wedding of Larry and Nancy Orrin. Larry had introduced me to OM at Asbury, and he had invited me to be best man at his wedding. It was the summer we were all to leave for the training conference in London. Our meeting in Florida was not a coincidence!

In reflection it may have seemed foolish and naive to accept the challenge Greg offered to me, but now after serving God for so many years, I can testify that He has proven Himself faithful. In reality everyone seems to be a fool for something or someone or for self. Rabid sports fans or fishermen, political party activists, Wall Street enthusiasts, selfish introspects, or family devotees are all fools for their causes whether they realize it or not. Magnify that list as you will. Whose fool are you?

Who is more worthy for us to be a fool for than the Lord Jesus Christ? I am not referring to any particular assumed Christian cause but to the person of Jesus Christ Himself — the suffering and resurrected Christ historically portrayed in Mel Gibson's classic film, *The Passion of the Christ.* It is He who is worthy of absolute obedience. The Apostle Paul wrote,

> *Let no one deceive himself. If anyone among you seems to be wise in this age, let him become a fool that he may become wise. For the wisdom of this world is foolishness with God* (1 Corinthians 3:18-19a).

The apostles were the central part of a team of believers whose purpose was to preach the Gospel and plant churches among the groups of people who knew little or nothing about the Lord. The Apostle Paul had fathered the church in Corinth. The believers there had become independent, rich, and arrogant. So Paul wrote to them,

> *I think that God has displayed us, the apostles, last, as men condemned to death; for we have been made a spectacle to the world, both to angels and to men. We are fools for Christ's sake, but you are wise in Christ! We are weak, but you are strong! You are distinguished, but we are dishonored! To the present hour we both hunger and thirst, and we are poorly clothed, and beaten, and homeless. And we labor, working with our own hands. Being reviled, we bless; being persecuted, we endure; being defamed, we entreat. We have been made as the filth of the world, the offscouring of all things until now* (1 Corinthians 4:9-13).

God was opening doors for us to follow in the footsteps of the apostles, to share the Gospel with people who lacked knowledge about our Lord Jesus Christ. After the summer conference our team set out for Spain. We were driving an old Volkswagon bus through the picturesque Pyrenees which divide France and Spain. I had a flashback to the year of my ROTC resignation. Then I had aspirations of driving a sleek green sports car in the southern mountain range of France decked in my Air Force officer's uniform. My mind was quickened with these words:

> 'For my thoughts are not your thoughts, neither are your ways my ways,' declares the Lord. As the heavens are higher than the earth, so are my ways higher than your ways and my thoughts than your thoughts (Isaiah 55:8-9 NIV).

I had a good plan for my life, but God had a higher purpose and a more abundant life!

We Americans especially are obsessed with happiness and what we think constitutes prosperity. So called Reality TV shows present extreme challenges and dare devil feats for money, fame, or just the thrill of doing something extraordinary. Could the idea Jesus proposed about abundant life be different than the American perspective? Jesus said,

> I have come that they might have life, and that they might have it more abundantly (John 10:10b KJV).

Fanatic young Muslims today are strapping plastic explosives to their bodies. They are motivated by hate. To kill as many people as possible is their goal. According to their teachings about the afterlife, abundance – including many virgins – awaits them for their sacrifice and martyrdom. What dedication they demonstrate for their cause!

As I read M. R. Narayan Swamy's *Inside An Elusive Mind — Prabhakaran*, I was astounded at the dedication and total commitment of the ethnic Tamil, Black Tigers, who are Hindus. They represent the terrorist's finest young people. They are the suicide squads of the separatist movement in Sri Lanka. Prabhakaran, the world's most ruthless guerrilla leader, has inspired them to blow themselves up along with the enemy for their dream of a separate country for Tamil people. On the other hand, love should motivate Christians to make such great sacrifices to bring eternal life to people. Jesus said, *Whoever finds his life will lose it, and whoever loses his life for my sake will find it* (Matthew 10:39 NIV).

Reverend A. W. Tozer, in one of his prophetic books written to stir up the sleeping American church, has a chapter entitled "Holiness before Happiness." We who are obsessed with happiness here and now are challenged by Tozer to rethink our philosophy in the light of eternity. Being a disciple for the Lord Jesus is not for the faint-hearted. Denying yourself and taking up your cross, losing your life in order to find it, loving your enemies, praying for those who despitefully use you, are all commands and challenges of the Holy Spirit inspired Word of God. To be a true disciple of Jesus is an extreme challenge and adventure with the promise of an abundant life.

Our team in the town of Caspe consisted of a Frenchman, a Belgian, a Mexican, and two Americans. We went from village to village and door to door selling the New Testament and various Christian books. In some places we were welcomed; in others doors were closed. Except for our Mexican brother, Willie Pena, our Spanish was severely limited. We had memorized enough phrases and sentences to sell books, but I think many people purchased them out of pity, amused at our broken Spanish. Nonetheless God's Word went forth.

I actually enjoyed Spain immensely. The thought of staying on for one year entered my mind. I could work with the university students in Madrid for many of them knew English. It would be so much easier than India which was a two-year commitment with OM. I could return to seminary a year sooner and finish my final year. Had I really heard God right? Did He really say, *Go to India?*

We had been told that Spain was the best experience of all the Western European countries in preparation for India. That proved true. On one of our excursions into the Spanish countryside we camped alongside a tree-lined stream. As the campfire dwindled to glowing embers in the early morning hours, I heard loud voices and a commotion outside. As I peered out the back window of our VW van where I had been sleeping, a sub-machine gun was pointed in my direction. The villagers had reported us to the police as possible bandits. After showing our passports and giving the officer-in-charge assurance that we were simply Christian booksellers, he warned us to be on the lookout. There were roving bandits reported in the vicinity.

We humans have the inclination to compromise or to take the path of least resistance. More often than not we shy away from sacrifice and discipline. We look for the easy way out. The Apostle Paul wrote a large portion of the New Testament. His life and discipline as a Christian has challenged and inspired millions throughout history. He wrote,

> *Do you not know that in a race all the runners run, but only one*
> *gets the prize? Run in such a way as to get the prize. Everyone*

who competes in the game goes into strict training. They do it to get a crown that will not last; but we do it to get a crown that will last forever. Therefore I do not run like a man running aimlessly; I do not fight like a man beating the air. No, I beat my body and make it my slave so that after I have preached to others, I myself will not be disqualified for the prize (1 Corinthians 9:24-27 NIV).

Soon afterward we stayed in a barn loft in Caspe. It had been renovated into a crude apartment good enough for some OM soldiers. We were foot soldiers for Jesus taking the Word into all the surrounding towns and villages. We became friends with the evangelical pastor who was a true Spaniard and his lovely German wife. They were a neat, stunning couple and were glad to have us minister with them. The church warmly appreciated our service to their community.

Throughout the summer of 1968 we systematically covered much of the Caspe area distributing thousands of New Testaments, Gospel packets, and tracts with a Bible correspondence course so that interested people could learn more about the Gospel. Billy Graham's book, *Paz Con Dios (Peace with God)* was a good seller. I often wonder how many Spaniards came to faith in Jesus after reading the literature we sold that summer. Only God knows.

Part of our daily routine on the team was a *quiet time*. This was our chance to study the Word of God, to read, and to pray. Christians who had given their life for the sake of the Gospel wrote many of the books I read. Their insights into the Word added fuel to the fire I felt burning in my heart. If Jesus Christ was the Only Begotten of the Father, the Son of God, and the Word become flesh (John 1:1), I could not be a half-hearted follower. It was all or nothing.

The Word of God became incredibly meaningful as we traveled around Caspe preaching and selling Christian literature. Jesus said, *I am the way, the truth, and the life. No one comes to the Father except through Me* (John 14:6). He gave a mandate to his followers:

All authority in heaven and on earth has been given to me. Therefore go and make disciples of all nations, baptizing them in the name of the Father and of the Son and of the Holy Spirit, and teaching them to obey everything I have commanded you. And surely I am with you always, to the very end of the age (Matthew 28:18b-20 NIV).

Not only was the Word coming alive, but we were learning a great deal by living together as an international team. Someone had rightly described the OM experience as a pressure cooker. We were a culturally diverse group of men but with the same Lord and with one purpose – to spread the Good News of Jesus Christ. He had risen from the dead. He was alive. There is hope after death and the promise of abundant life now. We discovered that Christianity works. His love was manifested in our relationship to each other. We were living out the New Testament pattern which is the Kingdom of God.

Early in September we returned to London. The summer recruits left for their respective countries, and we who were committed for the one or two year programs continued to study and prepare. Yes, I felt I had heard God speak to my heart while praying for spiritual reality, but did He really want me to go to India? Could it have been my sub-conscious mind only?

I was truly willing at this point, but Spain now was also an inviting option with only a one year break in my seminary studies instead of two. It was a needy place as well. Even the Roman Catholic Church had declared it a mission field since so few young people attended mass regularly. I prayed, "Lord, can you give me another confirmation that India is the place for me?" Over the next several days I forgot about that prayer and concentrated on learning all that I could about God, discipleship, and world evangelization.

One of the factors that contributed to my conviction that the Bible was inspired by God was the honesty of its reporting the shortcomings of His people. Moses was a great leader in Israel. He received the sacred tablets, the Ten Commandments, from the Lord Almighty but not before he complained that he was unable to speak well before people. He even lost his temper and killed an Egyptian and then went into hiding for years as a sheepherder in the desert.

Gideon was called by God to lead His people, Israel, against the Midianites. He knew what God wanted him to do, but still he desired a confirmation from God. Chapter six in the book of Judges tells the story of his asking God for assurance not once, not twice, but three times. He wanted confirmation too, just like us.

Most of the disciples were simple fishermen. Peter denied the Lord because of fear. James and John were referred to as "sons of thunder" because they wanted to call down fire from heaven on those who opposed them. Judas was a thief before he became the betrayer. Before his conversion the Apostle Paul was filled with hate and anger toward the Christians, hunting them down and consenting to their execution. Thomas was tagged as Doubting Thomas because he refused to believe unless he saw the resurrected Christ himself. After Pentecost Paul and Barnabas, founding fathers of the New Testament church, had an argument and formed two different teams. (Later they did reconcile.) I could relate to these men. They were ordinary people but with an extraordinary, loving, and merciful God.

I did not feel foolish or disobedient – just cautious. I rather liked Spain and could imagine a great year of ministry there. On the other hand India seemed so foreboding, so far away. As far as I was concerned, it was literally the "utter most parts of the earth".

In John chapter ten Jesus spoke as the good shepherd. Verse three says,

> He calls his own sheep by name and leads them out. When he has brought out all his own, he goes on ahead of them, and his sheep follow him because they know his voice.

OM leadership had assigned me to Spain because it was the best preparation for India. It was more "third world" than any other Western European country. I liked it. I wondered, *Would not God give me what I liked? Would He not give me something I was now familiar with? Wouldn't that be the abundant life?*

Our dining area at the London conference was a large gymnasium. Row after row of portable tables had been set up to accommodate a few hundred people. They were all covered with white plastic tablecloths, but underneath the plastic you could see newspaper. I sat down with some friends anticipating a good meal and fellowship. I also got a big laugh.

God has a sense of humor. Think about it. He spoke to Moses out of a burning bush (Exodus 3). He used a donkey to speak to the prophet Balaam (Numbers 22:21-41). He tells the sluggard to observe the ant and learn diligence (Proverbs 6:6).

God speaks through His creation.

> The heavens declare the glory of God: and the firmament shows His handiwork. Day unto day utters speech, and night unto night reveals knowledge. There is no speech nor language where their voice is not heard (Psalm 19:1).

He speaks through people.

> God, who at various times and in various ways, spoke in time past to the fathers by the prophets. . . . (Hebrews 1:1).

His message that day came to me through divine appointment. The tablecloth where I sat had not stretched completely over the underlying newspaper. There was a little space in which the newsprint was clearly visible. It was the *Personals* section. My eyes fell on the only complete ad that was visible between the two tablecloths. In bold letters it read:

Overland Trip to India

I am seeking someone to accompany me on
overland trip to India. If interested please contact. . . .

There were many tables in that large gymnasium. I just happened to sit at the table where this newspaper ad was right in front of me. Right! What are the odds of something like that happening by chance? Unimaginable! I chuckled to myself. "OK, God, I'm going to India."

November 16, 1968, we arrived at the border of Pakistan and India after descending down through the famous Khyber Pass from Afghanistan. It was my 25th birthday. Immigration police told us not to wander too far from the checkpoint. They reported that somewhere in the area were members of the Baluchi tribe who often shot first and asked questions later.

I was beginning to understand the clannish nature of Islam in these countries that esteem the Koran. I had already received a rifle butt to the chest when I complained to an Afghan soldier about what I thought was excessive road tolls. I quickly added, "No problem!" and paid the toll. These experiences proved to be portents of exciting trials and tribulations that awaited us in India.

At daybreak the timber gate weighed down with rocks tied to one end was lifted, and we rolled across the border into Punjab, a far north state in India. The heat was stifling. You could have fried an egg on the pavement. We had several hours of driving before reaching the capital of New Delhi and our base. Suddenly a loud BOOM! broke the monotony of the rattling diesel engine. I pulled to the side of the road and found that one of our rear tires had burst. The old British, Ford Thames truck was packed solid with supplies for India, used clothing, spare parts, and even a spare diesel engine.

I found some mechanics coveralls and slipped into them. At least my clothes would not be dirty when we arrived at the New Delhi OM headquarters. I found the jack and grabbed it in a hurry. Instead of the base handle I got hold of the greasy, grooved neck. Black, gritty gunk squeezed through my fingers and caked over my palm.

Crawling under the vehicle, I searched for a secure place to first wedge the jack and then begin turning the rod. Slowly the truck lifted off the ground enough to remove the flat. Sweat poured into my eyes as I lay sprawled on the dusty ground. I squinted trying to focus on what appeared to be moving shadows darting back and forth across the highway. From beneath the shade of the truck I stared down the road and soon realized that the mysterious moving shadows were masses of flies. It was disgusting.

Without thinking I wiped the sweat from my brow. Now the black grime painted my cheeks and forehead. I was totally frustrated and uncomfortable. Banging the lug wrench on the pavement I cried out, "Lord, is this abundant life?"

Immediately the answer came to my mind. "This is it, my son." I was flabbergasted. At the same time I intuitively knew something about the abundant life Jesus promised his disciples. That life does not depend on your circumstances. It is being confident that your name is written in the Lamb's Book of Life (Revelation 21:27). Concurrently it is the assurance that your life is lining up with God's priorities. You know God in an experiential way and He knows you because you are doing His will. His will is that everyone should be saved and come to the knowledge of the truth.

I had not gone to India for a vacation or an exciting adventure. I was there to help spread the Good News. My life was lining up with God's priority to reach the whole world even to the utter most places like India. Bob Sjogren wrote one of the books that I had read confirming God's will to reach the entire world. His book clearly shows the Father's will for all nations from Genesis through Revelation.

Years later I asked a nationally known American preacher if the Apostle Paul had this abundant life in the light of all that he suffered. Paul wrote,

> But we have this treasure in earthen vessels, that the excellence of the power may be of God and not of us. We are hard-pressed on every side, yet not crushed; we are perplexed, but not in despair; persecuted, but not forsaken; struck down but not destroyed (2 Corinthians 4:7-9).

The celebrity preacher quickly answered in the negative. "No, Paul did not have the abundant life as we have it today." I turned from the podium and started to walk away when the speaker offered a clarification as a second thought. "Well, he had it spiritually speaking but not in other ways." I knew instinctively that the preacher had a strictly Americanized view of the abundant life.

Underneath that truck with grease on my head, sweat in my eyes, and flies all around me, I had heard another word. "This is it, my son." God wanted to teach me something in India about the abundant life promised by Jesus. It was more in line with what Paul spoke of when he wrote,

> *Behold, now is the accepted time; behold now is the day of salvation. We give no offense in anything, that our ministry may not be blamed. But in all things we commend ourselves as ministers of God: in much patience, in tribulations, in needs, in distresses, in stripes, in imprisonments, in tumults, in labors, in sleeplessness, in fastings; by purity, by knowledge, by longsuffering, by kindness, by the Holy Spirit, by sincere love, by the word of truth, by the power of God, by the armor of righteousness on the right hand and on the left, by honor and dishonor, by evil report and good report; as deceivers, and yet true; as unknown, and yet well known; as dying, and behold we live; as chastened, and yet not killed; as sorrowful, yet always rejoicing; as poor, yet making many rich; as having nothing, and yet possessing all things* (2 Corinthians 6:2b-10).

The celebrity preacher had revealed the prevailing American perspective on abundant life which was not the reality that Jesus taught. They are diametrically opposed.

Another American preacher reported the euphoric feeling he had while driving down the California coastal highway in his sleek sports car talking on his cell phone. God is prospering him and his church is growing. The Word comes forth from his mouth with anointing, inspiring those who hear it. Does he have this abundant life? Possibly, but it is not because of his circumstances. If he has no world vision which actually involves him meaningfully in getting the Gospel to those still waiting to hear it for the first time, I dare to say he is being cheated by the enemy no matter how good he feels about his ministry and life. One great missionary said, "Why should some hear the Gospel over and over while others have never heard it even once?" Every Christian should reflect God's love for the *whole* world.

Assuredly not everyone is called to go to the ends of the earth, but all should be concerned and involved in the Great Commission of Jesus in some way. You can become knowledgeable enough to pray intelligently for areas in the world where the Gospel has not penetrated. You can pray for and support missionaries, Americans or national church planters in other countries. You can be a linking/helps ministry providing contacts for national ministries in the poorer countries to expand their outreach so more souls will be saved. Possibilities are limited only by our lack of genuine Holy Spirit inspired concern.

Terrorism is on a rampage throughout the world. Natural disasters like the tsunami of 2004 in the Indian Ocean, the successive hurricanes in the Gulf of Mexico, and the earthquakes, floods, and landslides around the world in 2005 are all indicators that we are living on borrowed time. In Matthew 24 Jesus said that there would be a great increase in natural disasters like these and then He went on to say,

> *And because lawlessness* (terrorism could easily be substituted here) *will abound, the love of many will grow cold. But he who endures to the end shall be saved. And this gospel of the kingdom will be preached in all the world as a witness to all the nations, and then the end will come* (Matthew 24:12-14).

When many or most hearts in the world are growing cold and apathetic, there still will be a remnant of God's people who will be active in the worldwide missionary adventure of getting the Good News to all the nations. *Ethnos* in the Greek denotes a distinct people group, nation, or tribe. I believe that this is the very heart of God. He will have a people who will worship him from *every tribe and language and people and nation. . . .*(Revelation 5:9b NIV). My hope is that this testimonial will confront you with a new dimension of Christian living in the light of God's plan for the nations. We are all called to *be* witnesses (Acts 1:8). Some will leave their homes for other places even to distant lands. Jesus calls His followers to pray for laborers to go forth into the harvest fields of the world (Matthew 9:36-38). It costs money to send out workers into the harvest fields, so giving is a vital aspect of the abundant life of Jesus as well.

Giving money is often the American cop-out for fulfilling the obligation of really getting involved. It is much easier and quicker to just write a check instead of committing yourself to at least a short term mission experience. Still, if God has called and enabled you to give, that may be your God given ministry.

Do not let Satan rob you of the experience of *going* when it is a viable option for your life. I assure you that God will enrich your life immeasurably when you abandon yourself to Him for the cause of taking the Gospel to all nations. If you are missing this global outlook in your Christian walk, I dare say that the enemy is robbing you of the full abundant life that Jesus promised.

Chapter

5

STUCK IN THE MUD

Calcutta is an intriguing city sprawled out along the Hooghly River which empties into the Bay of Bengal. Our OM base was a rented two-story house on a side street off Lower Circular Road, one of the main thoroughfares circumventing part of the city.

We had our team routine. Rising before daybreak we had calisthenics, followed by personal devotions, and then group devotions. The harmonium, tambourine, and Indian drum enhanced our worship and made it especially rhythmical and distinctively Asian. I loved it and was so much into the spirit of worship that I discovered an instrument of my own. The big wooden box on which I sat made a deep resonating bass sound. I beat it vigorously as the Indian brothers gleefully responded. God was bonding us and worship seemed to be the glue.

The Abundant Life Assembly of God was within walking distance from our base. When we had conferences with lots of extra people, Pastor Mark Buntain, whose love for Calcutta was obvious, made his church available for our meetings. The Carey Baptist Church was further away, but many of our OM teammates attended there also. That church was named in honor of the great pioneering missionary from England, William Carey. He translated the Bible into at least forty languages and is the one who inspired many with his statement, "Expect great things from God; attempt great things for God."

The churches in India, for the most part, appreciated our ministry. We were their foot soldiers carrying the Gospel message to the masses in the streets, the market places, and door to door.

Bihar was one of the most backward states in India, and I was assigned to the team that was to minister there. Most of our team members were from the state of Kerala on the southwest coast of the subcontinent.

They speak Malayalam. Tradition says that the Apostle Thomas established churches in south India in the first century, so there are many more Christians in the south than in the north. Many Christians also live in Chenai, the capital of Tamil Nadu, the state on the southeast coast. Their language is Tamil.

Our team leaders were A. T. Chacko and N. J. Varughese. I was the truck driver. The Indians could not legally drive the internationally registered trucks we had driven overland from England. Most of them at that time did not know how to drive anyway. Rudy Gomez, an Anglo-Indian from Calcutta whom we all grew to love dearly, was our literature man. I think his father was Indian and his mother British. Our team treasurer was M. A. Chandy also from Kerala. For a few months Giovanni, a short, stocky Italian helped me with the driving. The other two members were Jai Prakash, a slender, handsome, young Brahmin convert from Utter Pradesh, the most populace state in India, and S. N. Dass, a Hindu convert, who was from the state of Bengal where Calcutta is located.

We supported ourselves by selling Christian books, Gospel packets, Bibles, and New Testaments. We also sold good educational books and literary classics. After a day of selling on the streets and in the markets of Bihar, we handed all our sales money to the team treasurer, M. A. Chandy. He would do his bookwork – keeping only enough for our diesel, food, and necessities – and then would send a postal money order back to the base in Calcutta.

No one had any more than anyone else. If anyone had a need, he asked the treasurer for money. For example, it was not long before one of my Indian sandals broke. I had to ask for the money to purchase new ones. The American was drawing from the same source as the Indians, but I was not holding the purse. We slept side-by-side along the road. We ate the same food. We washed in the same rivers or at the same wells. We experienced true Christian community.

This was quite a contrast from my familiar environment in America. I left Dad and Mom, two brothers, and two sisters to travel with a team to the remote villages of northeast India. My family now included these Indian brothers and prayer partners back in America. I would never be the same. I was no longer just studying the New Testament in seminary. We were living the New Testament life together. I had prayed fervently for spiritual reality in my dormitory closet and God had set me in this place and position to learn it. It was His answer for my heart's desire.

I could identify with Peter who declared that the disciples had left everything to follow Jesus. The truth of Jesus' reply was becoming a reality for me.

> *I tell you the truth . . . no one who has left home or brothers or sisters or mother or father or children or fields for my sake and the Gospel will fail to receive a hundred times as much in this present age (homes, brothers, sisters, mothers, children and fields — and with them persecutions) and in the age to come, eternal life. But many who are first will be last, and the last first* (Mark 10:29-31 NIV).

Learning from the Indian brothers was a joy for me. If Jesus had simply taught some nice moral lessons and left it at that, I could have been off the hook and back enjoying the comforts at home in the United States. Buddhism has great moral teachings. Hinduism evokes fervent devotion to many gods. Muslims follow strict moral standards and pray to Allah five times a day. There were established religions and philosophies in Jesus' day also. Yet He commanded His disciples to go to the whole world, preach the Good News, and make disciples (Matthew 28:18-20).

I was curious about the conversions of my teammates. "You had your own religion. Why did you become a Christian?" Basically their answers were all the same. "Jesus. There was no Jesus Christ in our religion." It was the power in the person of Jesus Christ who said, *I am the way and the truth and the life. No one comes to the Father except through me* (John 14:6 NIV).

One Buddhist convert told me that Buddhism "has some excellent teachings but no life transforming experience with power to actually live by its doctrines. You are on your own to follow the teachings." He received Jesus Christ as Lord and Savior and was transformed. Now he is a highly respected Christian pastor in Colombo, Sri Lanka, and effectively communicates the Gospel to Sri Lankan Buddhists. I asked him why there has not been a greater number of Buddhists coming to faith in Christ like what is happening in Korea. Looking sad and serious, he said, "Many believe in Jesus Christ, but because of social pressure, they do not openly confess Him and take baptism. They would lose their standing in society and be shamed by their families."

Many Indian brothers paid a high price to follow Jesus. Like A. Stephen some had to leave home for fear of their lives. I learned much about sacrifice through them. Jesus said,

> *Do not suppose that I have come to bring peace to the earth. I did*

not come to bring peace, but a sword. For I have come to set 'a man against his father, a daughter against her mother, a daughter-in-law against her mother-in-law, and a man's enemies will be those of his own household.' He who loves father or mother more than me is not worthy of me. And he who loves his son or daughter more than me is not worthy of me. And he who does not take up his cross and follow me is not worthy of me (Matthew 10:34-38).

When I was initially tickled by God at the University of Tulsa, Campus Crusade for Christ channeled demographic information to us. Twelve thousand tribes or nations at that time had no viable Christian church or witness. The Indian sub-continent had the majority of those unreached peoples. The Van Deusen Letter distributed by Campus Crusade gave a stirring call to young Christians. I read the letter several times and accepted the challenge. Nothing was more important – nothing was more worthy of a lifetime commitment. Jesus gave the Great Commission in Matthew 28:16-20. That brought me to India, to Bihar, and to these tribal people.

Our team was assigned to work with a veteran British missionary in the Pallamau District of Bihar, a tribal area. I learned that India has more tribes or distinct ethnic groups than any country in the world.

My first crisis in India was about to clarify the meaning of the abundant life and the spiritual reality I was discovering. In our journey to Pallamau we came to a 'Y' in the road with an Indian Oil station at the intersection. The service attendant filled our diesel tank and advised me that only one headlamp was working. He had none of that type and was unable to replace it. He also told us that the road going to the left through the jungle was at least fifty miles shorter to our destination. We decided to take the shortcut. One hour later it began to rain. Light showers soon turned to a deluge, an early monsoon downpour.

Night came sooner than we anticipated, and my vision was impaired with just the one headlight. We came to the top of a hill. Looking down we saw a line of logging trucks pulled to the side of the dirt road. Their headlights were on and the engines were running but no one was moving. Chacko and I got down and walked over to a group of *satargees* standing alongside the road. They wore turbines around their heads and had beards.

Some of them were of the Sikh religion which was founded by Guru Nanak around the time Columbus discovered America. Nanak had rejected Hinduism and Islam but combined aspects of both with his writings. Sadhu Sundar Singh, a convert from that religion, was one of the greatest Christians of India and of all Christendom. He lived in the early nineteen hundreds in North India. Jesus appeared to Sundar Singh in a spectacular vision during a crisis in his young adult life. As a result, he became a wandering evangelist and ultimately disappeared in the Himalayan Mountains on a preaching mission to reach the unevangelized people of Tibet. His books reflect his deep faith in the Lord Jesus Christ. A movie based on his life was widely distributed to churches in America by Ken Anderson Films.

The truckers told us that a vehicle was being pulled from the ditch and that traffic should start moving again soon. They cautioned us that a normally dry riverbed at the bottom of the hill was filling up fast. Later the rain became incessant as Chacko and I stood on the rocky bank and stared across the river. The normally small stream had now widened to a fast flowing river. It looked fearsome as the traffic began to move, one truck crossing after another. I tried to chart the course, drawing a mental map of their ford.

We prayed and felt an assurance to go forward rather than turn back to the longer route around the jungle. We had been warned that the floodwaters had probably dug out some deeper holes on the riverbed. It was imperative that we follow the path of the trucks as closely as possible.

In those fearful moments I had time for both humor and a lesson in theology. Jesus never said, "I am a way." He said, *I am the way, the truth, and the life. No one comes to the Father except through Me* (John 14:6). I briefly thought of the Hindu premise that there are many ways to god and we all reach there sooner or later. I certainly could not trust that premise for crossing this river in the dark this night. There was a way across and I had to stick to that way. It was not only my life at stake. I had precious Indian brothers depending on me.

Though our backgrounds were vastly different, the Indian brothers each had a personal experience with the Lord Jesus. They each had been tickled in their own way. God was no longer an idol or simply a thought. Once, like Philip, they may have asked,

> Lord, show us the Father and that will be enough for us. Jesus answered, "Don't you know me, Philip, even after I have been among you such a long time? Anyone who has seen me has seen the Father. How can you say, 'Show us the Father? ((John 14:8 NIV)

My Indian brothers and I had found the same reality. Our relationship to the Father was the result of a relationship with Jesus Christ. Our shared faith made fellowship possible. 1 John 1:3 NIV states,

> *We proclaim to you what we have seen and heard, so that you also may have fellowship with us. And our fellowship is with the Father and with his Son, Jesus Christ.*

We as a team experienced unity because of the unity of the Father and the Son. Fellowship with the Father and fellowship with the Son go together. Scripture ties them together. Jesus prayed,

> *Now I am no longer in the world, but these are in the world, and I come to You. Holy Father, keep through Your name those whom You have given Me, that they may be one as We are one.*(John 17:11).

The riverbed was rocky. Some were really big rocks. The truck would suddenly shake and then drop. I was driving by faith with one headlight and believing that we would not drop off into a deep swirling pool and be swept off down stream. My body was tense. Though my faith was strong, it was being tested with every sudden jerk and sway of the truck.

We gave a united shout of joy as our front wheels hit solid ground. We had made it to the other side. Ten minutes later as we rounded a curve with dense jungle on either side, a rush of water was streaming down the hill and across the road. I made a split-second decision to drive through the muddy cascade. The steering wheel locked to the left. I had no control. The flash flood had washed away part of the road. Suddenly the truck lurched forward, and we were thrown into the side ditch, stuck in deep mud, and listing at nearly a forty-five degree angle. *What had I done? Our team was depending on me. I had let them down. Should I have taken more precaution? What would they think of me now?* Many questions roared in my mind.

No one was really hurt. We were all shaken up and bruised a little. Our wood literature crates had shifted. Some overturned. We were securely stuck in the mud, but there was no major damage to the truck. With difficulty we climbed out to assess the situation. As the rain began to let up, Chacko and I walked further down the road. I felt distressed and perplexed. Chacko lifted my spirit when he prayed. Assurance filled our hearts. Things would work out somehow.

This was our first major crisis in India as a team. It proved to be a Book of Acts experience. Jesus commissioned his disciples to go into all the world and make disciples. It was a hostile world. The Romans had built a good road system but not to every village and remote place. The

Apostle Paul wrote,

> But we have this treasure in jars of clay to show that this all-surpassing power is from God and not from us. We are hard pressed on every side, but not crushed; perplexed, but not in despair; persecuted, but not abandoned; struck down, but not destroyed. We always carrying around in our body the death of Jesus, so that the life of Jesus may also be revealed in our body (2 Corinthians 4:7-10 NIV).

The life of Jesus was to be shown through our bodies right here in the Bihar jungle. We were stuck in the mud, but we were being stretched in the spirit. We were deflated emotionally and mentally exhausted. What were we to do?

Chacko and I returned to the team after a long prayer walk. Everyone was bedding down for the night. Thank God the rain stopped. We had plastic sheets to cover the ground so that our sleeping bags and bedrolls would be protected from the moisture. Though we were all in the same boat, I did have one last vestige of my American culture – an air mattress. The Indian brothers had never seen one. They were used to sleeping on hard surfaces. I thought that was probably why they had such good postures and few back problems, but hard was not what I was used too.

I inflated it, spread my sleeping bag on top, and laid down. Adjusting my position a bit, a sudden menacing "poof" sound caused me further consternation. Slowly I sank to the damp cold ground. A stone had punctured my only remaining American comfort. *Is this abundant life?* was my unspoken question. God had many lessons to teach me about the life Jesus promised his disciples. He sent me to India for reeducation.

I began to think that we Western Christians are really pampered. We have been duped to think that American Christianity is the epitome of true Christianity. I was experiencing a peace with these Indian brothers by my side that was incomprehensible. The Apostle Paul wrote to the church in Thessalonica,

> Now may the God of peace Himself sanctify you completely; and may your whole spirit, soul, and body be preserved blameless at the coming of our Lord Jesus Christ (1 Thessalonians 5:23).

India was the environment for me to distinguish the difference between my mind, my emotions, my will, and my spirit. Amazingly it was also an Asian who became my teacher during this time through his book, *The Spiritual Man.* Watchman Nee was a Chinese Christian who suffered and died in a communist prison camp. This is the only one of his many books which he personally wrote. The others were all later transcribed from notes at his lectures.

In a sense we humans are all stuck in the mud. I feel sorry for those who believe they are simply an animal with a more developed brain, a cosmic accident of lightning striking an amoeba-like protein, or something equally strange. People who say they believe that do not really live that way unless they are ruthless and animalistic people, caring for no one except themselves. No! People who believe they have evolved to a more intelligent animal believe in love, and family, and purpose, or they cannot function in this life. They feel sadness when a loved one dies. They are not able to dismiss their loved one's life as just a cosmic accident returned to dust. We have eternity lodged in our minds.

The Bible tells us that God created man from the dust of the earth. He (God) *breathed into his nostrils the breath of life; and man became a living soul* (Genesis 2:7 KJV). We know that man's body will die and eventually decay and turn to dirt. Does it have any real value? A chemist told me that the human body is chemically worth only a few dollars except if there is gold in the teeth. Its value then depends on the price of gold at the time of death.

Listen again to the value God places on our bodies. Paul wrote to the Christians in the city of Corinth,

> *Do you not know that you are the temple of God and that the Spirit of God dwells in you? If anyone defiles the temple of God, God will destroy him. For the temple of God is holy, which temple you are* (1 Corinthians 3:16-17).

Luke, a medical doctor and author of the Acts of the Apostles, quotes Paul's exhortation to pastors – also referred to as overseers – of the first century church, *to shepherd the church of God which He purchased with His own blood* (Acts 20:28b). We Christians believe the Virgin Mary was overshadowed by God's Spirit and she conceived miraculously. We know scientifically that a person's blood genetically comes from the man and not the woman. Paul would be right scientifically. It was the very blood of God that flowed in the veins of Jesus Christ. Jesus Christ paid an unbelievable price for us to experience eternal life and abundant life now!

We are all stuck in the mud, but according to God it is precious mud beyond measure. The Hindus, I learned while in India, treat the body as *maya* or illusion. I saw Hindu holy men torture their bodies by lying on a bed of nails for days or have themselves buried in the hot beach sand under the baking sun thinking that this would help them escape the illusion and become one with god. It was all for personal benefit in a possible future life.

How different the Christian view is! Paul said,

> *I discipline my body and bring it into subjection, lest, when I have preached to others, I myself should become disqualified* (1 Corinthians 9:27).

It was for the sake of others that he disciplined his body. He wanted his preaching to be backed up with his righteous living. The hope of the Christian believer is that there is a place called heaven where Jesus Christ sits now at the right hand of Father God and He is preparing a place there for His children (John 14:2).

Mel Gibson's movie, *The Passion of the Christ*, graphically portrayed the actual price paid by Jesus Christ for our redemption so that we would have the blessed hope of being with Him after death. Jesus did not agonize for us so that we then would have to go off into a "soul sleep" for endless ages until he returns to planet Earth. No, the Scripture says as far as our bodies are concerned they are asleep until He comes. His agony and death, however, bound us who believe so intimately to Him that even without a human body we will be with Him. 1 Thessalonians 5:10 says He, *died for us, that whether we wake or sleep, we should live together with Him.*

Stuck in this mud as we are, there is a deep confidence that believers have in facing death. Paul reveals this in 2 Corinthians 5:8. *We are confident, yes, well pleased rather to be absent from the body, and to be present with the Lord.* The Apostle Paul expressed a very human feeling when he wrote, *I desire to depart and be with Christ, which is better by far* (Philippians 1:23). It is far better for the believer, but it is not yet the best in every way. John Piper points out in chapter 40 of his book, *The Passion of Christ,* that "Sleep-like, the body lies there in the grave. But we live with Christ in heaven. This is not our final hope. Someday the body will be raised. But short of that, to be with Christ is precious beyond words."

God had many lessons to teach me about the abundant life which Jesus promised His disciples. The jungle was home to dangerous animals, tigers, wild elephants, and poisonous snakes. The sounds of the night kept my one eye open, yet we found His mercies new as morning sun flickered through the trees. Psalm 30:5 says,

> *For His anger is but for a moment, his favor is for a lifetime;*

weeping may endure for the night, but joy comes in the morning.

Early the next morning a logging truck came upon us as we aroused from our fitful sleep. The loggers soon had us out of the ditch. As they unloaded and reloaded our precious cargo, I noticed a couple of them sneaking Bible portions into their pockets. The Word of God was going out! Psalm 126:6 says,

He who goes out weeping, carrying seed to sow, will return with songs of joy, carrying sheaves with him (NIV).

The privilege of laying trophies at His feet – men and women we have helped lead to Christ – makes living in this fallen world worthwhile. That's abundant life!

Chapter
6

END OF THE ROAD

"Lord, we are all dried up. We have no strength to carry on. We have little diesel left and no money. We have come to the end of the road." That was the depressing prayer of Rudy Gomez, our literature man. This was his natural temperament. He tended to be rather melancholic which was possibly inherited by his background as an Anglo-Indian growing up in Calcutta. On the other hand, he was truthful, or should I say factual? He had his facts right and was honest enough to tell God how we all felt.

We were silent after Rudy's prayer. Each of us felt a horrible spiritual oppression in this place. It was stifling. The heaviness, I imagined, was like having your head in a vice. You could actually feel pressure. Only the occasional haunting whistle of the pheasant crow interrupting the continuous buzz of the summer cicada, often called locusts in the midwest, reminded me that this was not actually hell.

We had arrived safely at our planned destination, Baudh, Orissa south of Bihar along the Bay of Bengal. Baudh was a large town literally at the end of a single lane paved road. Even the name sounded foreboding. We were told there were more Hindu temples and shrines in Orissa than in any other state in India. Here we intended to preach the Gospel and sell Bibles, New Testaments, and Gospel packets.

Upon our arrival we saw Hindu festival wagons parked along the main street. Their giant, brightly painted, wooden wheels looked to be at least ten feet high. Indian mythology created auspicious days to celebrate events pertaining to the gods. During the celebration of a god's festival that particular god would be enthroned and garlanded atop the wagon platform. It was then pulled through the streets to the local reservoir, placed on a miniature wooden raft, and launched on the water surrounded by burning candles. Sometimes it was pulled by men who had placed themselves in a trance and had large meat hooks pierced through the skin on their back and tied to the wagon. No blood was visible coming from the wounds, but the skin was stretched grotesquely out from the torso as the devotee pulled the god along slowly. The gods glowed in the night as the idol raft drifted toward a watery grave some distance from the shore. This was repeated year after year.

Ron Penny, an Englishman, was our regional coordinator. He had recalled our team leader, Divakaran, to Calcutta and given him another assignment. Since I had the most experience – which wasn't much – he assigned me to lead the team in Baudh. Actually I had been on an Indian team for just one year. This was a historic team in one sense. Pran and Danajaha Nyack joined us and were the first recruits from Orissa to work with OM. Of course, they knew the Oriya language which was completely different than Hindi. Though we had Oriya literature, only Divakaran knew the language before Pran and Nyack arrived.

India is a very complex country. There are an estimated seventeen hundred languages and dialects. The Indian brothers grew up hearing two or three languages spoken daily and sometimes more. They have a natural aptitude for languages that we Americans lack. Pran and Nyack not only knew the language, but they were full of fresh fire. They refreshed us just like the Apostle Paul wrote about Philemon refreshing the hearts of the saints (Philemon v.7).

Our first morning in Baudh, however, was as dry as the Rajasthani desert in the Indian northwest. What were we to do? There were no churches anywhere near the area, and there were no Christians that we were aware of. India officially has only about three per cent Christians but this state reported only a fraction of one percent. None of us were thinking of statistics though – just surviving.

After Rudy's deflated prayer there was silence for quite some time. Then I prayed, "Lord, what Rudy prayed seems to be the case. We have no strength in ourselves. We feel depressed with this place and situation. But, Lord, you said to go to the ends of the world and preach and make disciples. We are here at the end of the road and at the end of ourselves because we want to be obedient to your command. Help us, Lord, to share the Word with these people whom you love."

As I continued praying, I began to pray the Scriptures which came to my mind, "Lord, you are the true vine, and the Father is the vine dresser. Every branch in you that does not bear fruit the Father takes away; and every branch that bears fruit the Father prunes that it may bear more fruit. Lord, we are clean because of the word which you have given us and now we abide in you and you abide in us. This morning we *choose* to abide in you and let you abide in us. You said that we would bear much fruit by abiding in you and apart from you we can do *nothing*. The ministry is in your hands. Amen." I was numb but I meant what I prayed. It was the Word of God from John 15.

I do not recall that I had been taught to pray Scriptures. It just came out. Much of the Scriptures were now increasingly in my mind. They had become my life in India when my feelings were repulsed by all the idolatry, the lack of sanitation, poverty, and masses of people everywhere. As the Scriptures became my life, I noticed that my thinking was influenced proportionately.

After prayer, still emotionally numb, we arose and paired off. Mark 6:7-8 was our example.

> *And He* (Jesus) *called the twelve to Himself, and began to send them out two by two, and gave them power over unclean spirits. He commanded them to take nothing for the journey except a staff – no bag, no bread, no copper in their money belts. . . .*

Not only were we in a spiritual desert at the end of the road, we were out of money. That is depressing. Poverty certainly is a curse. We were not really poor though for we had the Word of God! Our aim was to sell it to the Hindus, and thus we would have money to buy diesel, food, and all that we needed. We had to trust that the people of Baudh would buy our Gospel packets, Bibles, and New Testaments, or any other books that we carried. Like the disciples we were going out without money. The New Testament was being acted out.

The Bible that we have is not translated directly from the original manuscripts, but the God who inspired those originals also used fallible man to transcribe copies and keep His Word completely reliable even to this day. What we were experiencing at the end of the road was exactly the thesis of this book. Our spiritual knowledge was growing through our personal experiences of the Word. We were discovering that God's truth is real. Watchman Nee, while incarcerated in a communist prison, realized that it is the union of the believer's life with truth (Jesus) that brings genuine spiritual knowledge. God has not wound up the universe and moved away. No! He is ever present to those who trust Him. *Jesus Christ is the same yesterday and today and forever* (Hebrews 13:8 NIV).

We had traveled here in faith. Now we had to trust – to rely confidently on Him to do what He promised. After you have done everything in faith, it is time to trust. God was teaching us many things. OM training is often called the pressure-cooker. We understood! It was literally very hot in India most of the time, but the real pressure we were under was the pressure to trust Him without reservation. We certainly were not trusting in our emotions. We were beyond frustration. Now was the time for raw obedience. The Great Commission had not been revoked. According to Jesus our love for Him would be demonstrated by our obedience. *If you love me, you will keep my commandments* (John 14:15).

Something very significant and seemingly extraordinary happened as we walked two by two into the town. With every step I felt increasing inner strength. Courage welled up in my heart. The countenance of our brothers began to change. Frustrated, weary frowns gave way to strained smiles and finally spontaneous grins.

Once I asked the Lord what I could do to praise Him more and be more effective in following Him. He seemed to answer in my heart, "to live for Me is to praise Me, and obedience is better than sacrifice." Our raw obedience to His Word was bringing life, peace, and joy in the midst of darkness all around us. I know now that depression can be lifted by being obedient and putting on *the garment of praise for the spirit of heaviness* (Isaiah 61:3b). The result is clear as Isaiah continues, *That they may be called trees of righteousness, the planting of the LORD, that He may be glorified* (Isaiah 61:4). India was fertile ground to grow us as trees of righteousness and we understood more and more that all glory goes to Him.

There is great liberation in abandonment to Jesus Christ who is the Word become flesh. The Word of God is alive.

> *For the word of God is living and powerful, and sharper than any two-edged sword, piercing even to the division of soul and spirit, and of joints and marrow, and is a discerner of the thoughts and intents of the heart* (Hebrews 4:12).

We were learning that Proverbs 3:5-6 were more than nice memory verses.

> *Trust in the LORD with all your heart, and lean not on your own understanding. In all your ways acknowledge Him, and He will make your paths straight* (NIV).

We had widely diverse theological traditions represented on our team, but our unity and reality of *koinonia* or fellowship was actual fact.

God, our Father, revealed that He is greater than any human thought about Him. Words may produce very opinionated, bigoted, religious people. But if you have abandoned yourself to the Word, at the end of the road when you have nothing else and are standing stripped of all pretensions, you can know that God is real and His truth is absolute.

Out of simple obedience, against the swelling and ebbing tides of emotion or intellectual debate, the Word swayed us. God was working in us the very attitude of Jesus Christ Himself.

Contrary to our expectations, Baudh became a spiritual oasis for the team. We discovered one Christian family there and had church in their home. It was a glorious time of discovering the Word becoming flesh and dwelling with us. There were several children in that family. The father and mother were both radiant Christians and each child reflected the same love and joy we saw in their parents. The contrast between this Christian family and the idol worshipping Hindus was striking and unquestionable.

Your countenance really does mirror the god or gods you worship and serve. We saw people who worshipped snakes and their eyes reminded you of snake eyes. Some worshipped monkeys and their actions reflected it. We saw rats being accommodated in some temples and the temple attendants resembled the same breed. Grotesque idols with monster like heads created fearful and superstitious followers. You do become what you worship. *For as he thinks in his heart, so is he* (Proverbs 23:7 NIV).

We met an old Hindu priest who chanted a mantra for hours to chase away evil spirits and perhaps gain merit. Fear was his primary felt emotion. Before he died, the bearded old man with glazed eyes received the Lord Jesus and salvation. The change in his countenance was dramatic. He did not look like the same person. His eyes were soft without that empty glare. There was an obvious aura of peace around his gently smiling face. 2 Corinthians 5:17 (NIV) says, *Therefore, if anyone is in Christ, he is a new creation; the old has gone, the new has come!*

Baudh was literally the end of the road. Even the Indian brothers had never been to such a remote and spiritually dark place. It was as great a culture shock for them coming from south India as it was for me coming from America. God has a way of getting deep into your psyche when you find yourself in a completely foreign culture. Your faith is stretched beyond your imagination. You are forced to trust Him when all your human senses cry "unfamiliar!" You learn perseverance and discover that He really is reliable. The Word of God becomes real nourishment for your soul, filled with glory.

You become more enthusiastic about the Word. I found myself shouting at times in the open-air markets. "Good News. Good News. Come and get your Good News." Many times my pockets bulged with rupees as curious eager buyers wanted to read this Good News for themselves. James 1:2-4 (NIV) says,

> *Consider it pure joy my brothers, whenever you face trials of many kinds, because you know that the testing of your faith develops perseverance. Perseverance must finish its work so that you may be mature and complete, not lacking anything.*

Young people today are risking their lives for cheap thrills. The highs of drugs, sex, and worldly entertainment are paltry substitutes for the adventure of being a true disciple of Jesus Christ. Sorry to say the church has tried to compete using similar worldly attractions and lost. Coke does not have the 'Real Thing.' The Church has the real thing in Jesus Christ but has often failed to proclaim Him and challenge young people to lay down their lives for Him.

Jesus issued an invitation to everyone to experience an extreme adventure with assured success. Jesus said,

> *If anyone would come after me, he must deny himself and take up his cross daily and follow me. For whoever wants to save his life will lose it, but whoever loses his life for me will save it* (Luke 9:23-24 NIV).

King David understood the inquiring mind and the searching heart when he wrote,

> *Taste and see that the LORD is good; Blessed is the man who trusts in Him!* (Psalm 34:8)

You *will* be blessed. The father of that Christian family in Baudh, Orissa, had built a spiritual oasis in an alien environment. I do not remember what was preached that Sunday as we worshipped in his home, but one of the Indian brothers gave the father a word of encouragement. I did not forget that! It was Psalm 127 (NIV).

> *Unless the Lord builds the house, its builders labor in vain. Unless the Lord watches over the city, the watchmen stand guard in vain. In vain you rise early and stay up late, toiling for food to eat — for He grants sleep to those he loves. Sons are a heritage from the Lord, children a reward from Him. Like arrows in the hands of a warrior are sons born in one's youth. Blessed is the man whose*

quiver is full of them. They will not be put to shame when they contend with their enemies in the gates.

That Psalm was a wonderful comfort to the Baudh Christian father. He had allowed the Lord to build his house. He was blessed with children who loved the Lord as he did. I learned much through the example of Christians like him in India. They were victorious and kept the joy of the Lord despite suffering persecutions, hardships, and being surrounded by idolatry. George Verwer speaks volumes when he says, "We learn the deepest lessons when we are out of our comfort zones."

My earnest prayer and motive for writing this book is that young people and young adults will accept this challenge of Jesus and find the extreme adventure. Likewise I pray that older generations will encourage them in their abandonment to the Kingdom of God. We all face the ultimate end of the road of our earthly existence. There is no better time than now to start laying up treasures in heaven.

SURROUNDED

Near the Nepali border we encountered some strong opposition. Our truck was parked along the main road just outside of town. Roads and streets in India are always crowded with people, cattle, bullock carts, bicycles, cars, motorcycles, and mangy dogs. Big trucks blast their horns and somehow make their way through the confused throngs. Many cover their faces with a handkerchief to keep from breathing the black diesel exhaust being spewed out from the buses and other vehicles threading their way through the masses.

We lowered the tailgate which we used as a preaching platform. Curious crowds began to press in around us as we started to sing, *"Kushi, Kushi, Maano. Kushi Kushi Maanoa."* A couple of brothers shook tambourines. The Hindi song spoke about being happy that Jesus died and rose again. For most of our listeners it was the first time they had heard the Good News. It was the first time many had heard the name Jesus.

I asked one old man if he knew who Jesus was. "No," he replied, "he doesn't live in this village, but I think he lives in the next town." One young man thought that we were from the Peace Corps and had come to introduce a hybrid rice called Jesus. There were some churches scattered throughout the northeast Indian interior in the late sixties, but Christianity was basically considered a foreign religion. Missiologists had named this area "The Graveyard of Modern Missions." From what I observed, that title fit.

The churches were usually surrounded by tall compound walls which echoed the failed mission strategy of the nineteenth century. Cathedral-like churches were constructed and traditional western or European type Christianity was propagated. It was not Indian. In that sense it was foreign.

Superstition and warped ideas of the Christian message made this area a hotbed of fanatic opposition.

When the singing and preaching ceased, we mingled with the crowd hawking the Good News of Jesus. In addition to New Testaments and Bibles we were selling Billy Graham's book, *Peace with God,* which had been translated into the Hindi language. A young man asked me to show him the book so I handed him a copy. Several of his buddies were standing around with him. The crowd was becoming restless. A ground swell of chatter sent shivers up my spine. Gathering onlookers around our truck began rumbling. The youthful inquirer's face grimaced as he flipped through the pages with a cursory, disinterested glance.

At that instant I realized that his comrades were encircling me. I was surrounded. Suddenly he ripped the book and flung the pieces above his head. The crowd was a hair's breath from becoming a mob. Fear enveloped my heart. *Was I about to die?* I wondered. An angry mob can ignite in an instant and trample everything in its path like a stampede of wild elephants.

Spontaneously the fear faded into a great peace. *Oh*, I thought, *I'm going to be with the Lord.* Motives are clarified in moments of impending danger and crisis. *Why had I come to India? Why was it so important to preach Jesus in this hostile area? They already had a religion.* Numerous such thoughts whizzed through my mind.

I knew in my heart love was the answer. Love was the motive that brought us. The Scriptures say,

> *God is love. Whoever lives in love lives in God, and God in him. In this way, love is made complete among us so that we will have confidence on the day of judgment, because in this world we are like Him. There is no fear in love. But perfect love drives out fear, because fear has to do with punishment. The one who fears is not made perfect in love. We love because He first loved us* (1 John 4:16-19 NIV).

God's love cast out the fear that had momentarily paralyzed me. Astonishingly and against my natural instinct I gently took the arm of the fuming lad and walked with him through the circle of his surprised friends as I naively questioned, "Why did you do that? It's a very good book and we have many different kinds which I will show you." I led him through the crowd up to the tailgate. Then I handed him several books of assorted titles.

This incident reminded me of when the angry mob surrounded Jesus because of His preaching. They,

> *rose up and thrust Him out of the city; and they led Him to the*
> *brow of the hill on which their city was built, that they might*
> *throw Him down over the cliff. Then passing through the midst of*
> *them, He went His way* (Luke 4:29-30).

By that time our whole team was aware of the danger. Slowly they made their way to the truck and began to pack up. Any signs of panic on our part would have inevitably ignited the volatile situation. We pulled away without injury and were rejoicing that the Word went out despite the opposition. The Acts of the Apostles is the record of how the church of Jesus Christ grew after the promised Holy Spirit came upon the 120 waiting disciples. It is a record of continually being surrounded by opposition and yet always pressing to take the Good News to more souls.

We were not being paid a big salary to be there preaching. On the contrary, we had invested our own money. We were not fulfilling our religious obligation in order to gain merit with an autocratic and distant god. We were simply sharing the message of hope and salvation found only in Jesus Christ.

> *Salvation is found in no one else, for there is no other name under*
> *heaven given to men by which we must be saved* (Acts 4:12 NIV).

We were confidently and joyously preaching the Good News of a resurrected Savior without apology. We were not sent to debate but to declare. It is true that you cannot prove the existence of God, but He proves Himself. We were not preaching our opinions but what God had revealed – Jesus, the human revelation of what God is really like. Hebrews 1:3 describes the Son,

> *Who being the brightness of His glory and the express image of*
> *His person, and upholding all things by the word of His power,*
> *when He had by Himself purged our sins, sat down at the right*
> *hand of the Majesty on high.*

Dr. E. Stanley Jones enjoyed quoting a little Italian slum-dwelling boy who, when asked by a teacher what he thought of Jesus, replied, "Jesus is the best photograph that God ever had took." Our team had come to this hostile place to present that very picture of God. Our lives were on the altar. We were living for Him who died for us. The Apostle Paul wrote,

> *If we are out of our mind, it is for the sake of God; if we are in our*
> *right mind, it is for you. For Christ's love compels us, because we*
> *are convinced that one died for all, and therefore all died. And he*

died for all, that those who live should no longer live for themselves
but for him who died for them and was raised again (2 Corinthians
5:13-15 NIV).

There are more than 630,000 villages in India. Many are remote
and still without electricity. The regular village markets are a lifeline for
the people. Naturally we targeted these gatherings to reach more people
for the Lord.

Another angry mob confronted us in a place called Tikaballi. India's
states are divided into districts that have daily markets in various locations.
People walk for miles to sell or barter their wares or produce. They sit
under thatched roofs supported by poles with the goods spread out before
them on plastic sheets, straw mats, or old newspapers. We circulated
two by two through the market when suddenly lots of noise errupted
from near the place where we had parked. When my teammate and I
emerged from the sprawling peddlers, we saw a large group of men
yelling at the other brothers. A few hecklers who were determined to
chase us from the market had incited them.

I confronted the leaders. "This is a free country," I said. "You can
preach and teach about Krishna or any god you want. So we are telling
the people about the Savior, Jesus Christ." Hinduism is a very syncretistic
religion. Everyone has his or her favorite god. There are millions. You
can buy a framed picture of your god even in these outside markets. The
picture of Jesus in a neat wooden frame was there too with his heart
exposed in His chest. To them He was just another addition to the mythical
pantheon.

The angry crowd would not listen to my appeal. Finally, I said, "OK,
we will leave for now." As we pulled away, the animosity poured out on
a local believer. We saw them beating him on the road. Later that night
we visited him in his village. He was bruised and swollen but happy. "It is
all right to take a beating for Jesus," he said.

It was a joy to meet some of God's choicest veteran missionaries
laboring in these difficult and resistant areas. Graham and Gladys Staines
were among the few foreign missionaries still in the northeast. They worked
with lepers at a clinic in Mayurbhanj, Orissa. That particular Australian
mission had been functioning in India for over one hundred years.

Graham was a godly man who lived very simply with his family on
the mission compound where we made our base for a couple of weeks.
He was a respected member of the local Rotary Club in Baripada and
peddled his old bike around town and to the monthly meetings.

Our original team leader, Brother Divakaran, knew Gladys and Graham before they met. Gladys was on one of our OM teams, and she was also from Australia. Divakaran thought this would be a good match so he asked permission to introduce them. Providentially, Gladys and Graham came to realize that they grew up in Australia living only about thirty miles from each other. God brought them together in India for the very first time. They married and had three children in India.

In early 1999 we received a phone call from our dear Indian brother N. J. Varughese. He reported that Graham and his two sons, Phillip (9) and Timothy (7) had been ambushed by a frenzied mob with flaming torches and were burned alive in Manoharpur, Orissa, India. Within six weeks Varughese and I journeyed to the mission compound to see how we could help Gladys.

She was remarkably peaceful and confident. The police were still interrogating her in search of reasons for the unspeakable tragedy. Gladys had received consoling letters from all over India and around the world and handed us one that had arrived by special courier from New Delhi, the capital of India. It was from Sonja Ghandhi, wife of the late Prime Minister Rajiv Gandhi, who was assassinated by Tamil Tigers from Sri Lanka. Muslims and Hindus were apologetic for what had happened to the Staines. They denied any sympathy for this fanatical and utterly hateful act.

Gladys asked us to help her with the correspondence, so we worked for hours drafting a form letter, signing for her, and finally posting them. This may not seem like exciting work but we knew we were fulfilling God's purpose in serving her in this way. A missionary is first of all a servant and no work is mundane when it is God-given. At this time she also asked us to go with her to the actual scene of the crime which she had not yet visited. After some hesitancy and a few phone calls, the police in charge of the investigation agreed to take her with special police escort. Throughout the three hour ride to Manoharpur people lined the road at various intersections to get a glimpse of the missionary widow who had been so much in the headlines. Apparently the word had gotten out that we were coming.

The ground was scorched black just outside the little white, mud-wall church. Father and the two sons had decided to sleep that night in their old Land Rover parked next to the church. Just after midnight they were attacked by a group of outsiders who had been riled up by a criminal who had targeted the missionary and planned the ambush. Later the

83

charred bodies and burnt out vehicle appeared in India's news headlines. I still have the *India Times* magazine that shows the gruesome photographs.

We held a special church service, and I preached a message on John 12:24,

> *Most assuredly, I say to you, unless a grain of wheat falls into the ground and dies, it remains alone; but if it dies, it produces much grain.*

Gladys and her sister visiting from Australia sat on the floor in the rear of the church with the other hundred or so believers. We all were aware of the sustaining presence of God and the comfort of His Word.

I asked some villagers about what they saw and heard that night. They said that the intruders shouted out in the street that everyone was to stay in their houses and lock the doors or they would be harmed. Because there is no electricity, it was very dark and there was lots of shouting and confusion. Some described seeing beams of light shining up into the night sky and hearing beautiful voices singing. Some thought that this might be angels singing and heaven's gates opening for the martyrs. I know what the Bible says about those who have suffered *in faith* for godly purposes.

> *Who through faith subdued kingdoms, worked righteousness, obtained promises, stopped the mouths of lions, quenched the violence of fire, escaped the edge of the sword, out of weakness were made strong, became valiant in battle, turned to flight the armies of the aliens. Women received their dead raised to life again. Others were tortured, not accepting deliverance, that they might obtain a better resurrection. Still others had trial of mockings and scourgings, yes, and of chains and imprisonment. They were stoned, they were sawn in two, were tempted, were slain with the sword. They wandered about in sheepskins and goatskins, being destitute, afflicted, tormented — of whom the world was not worthy. They wandered in deserts and mountains, in dens and caves of the earth. And all these, having obtained a good testimony through faith, did not receive the promise, God having provided something better for us, that they should not be made perfect apart from us. Therefore we also, since we are surrounded by so great a cloud of witnesses, let us lay aside every weight, and the sin which so easily ensnares us, and let us run with endurance the race that is set before us, looking unto Jesus,*

the author and finisher of our faith, who for the joy that was set before Him endured the cross, despising the shame, and has sat down at the right hand of the throne of God (Hebrews 11:33-40, 12:1-2).

Within a few months Gospel Literature Service of Mumbai, India had published a book, *Burnt Alive*, which I have enthusiastically distributed. It is the true story of the Staines family and the God whom they love and serve. The President of India at that time, K. R. Narayanan, is quoted at the beginning of the book. "That someone who spent years caring for patients of leprosy, instead of being thanked and appreciated as a role model should be put to death in this manner is a monumental aberration from the traditions of tolerance and humanity for which India is known. (It is) a crime that belongs to the world's inventory of black deeds."

The exclusive claim of Jesus Christ grates against the liberal claim that "all religions are equally true and valid and there are no absolutes." Hostile opposition surrounds true believers in Jesus Christ. Paul wrote,

whose minds the god of this age has blinded, who do not believe, lest the light of the gospel of the glory of Christ, who is the image of God, should shine on them (2 Corinthians 4:4).

Paul was probably the greatest missionary of all times. He wrote in Romans 15:20 *And so I have made it my aim to preach the gospel, not where Christ was named, lest I should build on another man's foundation.* No, like a true pioneer missionary he was compelled by the love of God to go to places where Christ was not known. In doing so he suffered much.

He describes his situation in 2 Corinthians 6:4-10,

In much patience, in tribulations, in needs, in distresses, in stripes, in imprisonments, in tumults, in labors, in sleeplessness, in fastings; by purity, by knowledge, by longsuffering, by kindness, by the Holy Spirit, by sincere love, by the word of truth, by the power of God, by the armor of righteousness on the right hand and on the left, by honor and dishonor, by evil report and good report; as deceivers, and yet true; as unknown and yet well known; as dying, and yet behold we live; as chastened and yet not killed; as sorrowful, yet always rejoicing; as poor, yet making many rich; as having nothing, and yet possessing all things.

India, I discovered, was home to some of the keenest Christian thinkers and preachers I had ever met. Many believers who were of noble character and deep faith became close friends. Their faith had been forged out of a crucible of dark mythological hodgepodge and illogical and circuitous philosophies. The end of all the religion in India as everywhere is simply words. How different is Jesus Christ!

> *And the Word became flesh and dwelt among us, and we beheld His glory, the glory as of the only begotten of the Father, full of grace and truth* (John 1:14).

Christians, those who have Christ dwelling in them and are following Him, are strangers and pilgrims in the world. Peter exhorts believers to live that way and to abstain from fleshly lusts which war against the soul (1 Peter 2:11). He further exhorts,

> *Beloved, do not think it strange concerning the fiery trial which is to try you, as though some strange thing happened to you; but rejoice to the extent that you partake of Christ's sufferings, that when His glory is revealed, you may also be glad with exceeding joy* (1 Peter 4:12-13).

As I walked down the street in Baripada, I wondered why people were staring so intently. A man stopped me and said that he had been a good friend of Graham Staines. He also was a fellow Rotarian in the same club. He was a Hindu, but Graham's death and the death of his two sons had greatly impacted his life. He mistook me for Graham's brother. Later when I saw photos at the mission house I realized that we had the same features, and I was wearing an Indian Nehru collar shirt like he always wore.

Gladys chose to stay on in India and continue the work among the lepers. She has forgiven the murderers and looks forward to the reunion with her family in heaven. The Negro slaves in America used to sing a spiritual song that had this line, "This world is not my home, I'm just 'a passin' through." Like Gladys and the slaves,

> we *know that the whole creation groans and labors with birth pangs together until now. Not only that, but we also who have the firstfruits of the Spirit, even we ourselves groan within ourselves, eagerly waiting for the adoption, the redemption of our body* (Romans 8:22-23).

Despite many daily victories in India, tons of Gospel literature being distributed, and the Good News being preached to previously unevangelized masses, I was growing weary and about to make the biggest mistake in my life.

Chapter
8

Surrendered

India assaulted all my senses. There were no public toilets in most of the towns and villages. People would urinate in the open, along a road or against a wall. In the early morning people could be seen walking along the road with a can or some kind of container filled with water. They were looking for a place to relieve themselves. Jesting with the brothers I coined the expression, "walls of urination and the fields of defecation." They understood my English and my anguish. There was no toilet paper. The water people carried did the job with the help of the left hand. I discovered that was the reason no one ate with their left hand. It was considered unclean even when you washed thoroughly with soap.

No one ate rice with utensils. You used your right hand. Eventually I learned the art of rolling the rice up into a ball and flicking it with my thumb into my mouth. We seldom used plates. The rice was dumped on large green banana leaves or smaller leaves sown together with thread-like vines. Different kinds of curries were plopped on or beside the mound of rice. These were made with exotic spices and usually included tomatoes, onions, potatoes, okra or eggplant. A thick lentil soup called *dawl* topped the rice and was very tasty. Though I acquired an affinity for Indian cuisine, I sometimes hankered for steak, mashed potatoes, and American fast food.

I found the Indian fast food to be "chickens on the run." Let me share an example. We camped in a jungle near a village. There was no restaurant or even a food shop nearby. One family saw our books and wanted a Bible and New Testament. They had no money to purchase them so we made a deal. Chickens were running through the bushes and around their house scratching the ground for bugs and worms. We offered them a Bible for a big rooster and a New Testament for a smaller hen.

They delightfully agreed but we had to catch our dinner. What a sight it was! I remember darting through the brush, diving for a terrified, squawking chicken. We were finally successful and made the trade.

We hired a local man to cook rice for us and make chicken curry while we distributed Gospel tracts and sold literature in a nearby market. It was dark when we returned to our campsite. We were very hungry and looked forward to the meal that had been prepared for us. Rice this time was served in white ceramic bowls. The chicken curry was also served in the same kind of bowl. When I reached into the gravy to get a piece of meat, I pulled out a foot, toes and all. Tossing it to a drooling dog at my feet, I reached for another piece of meat in my bowl. This time my fingers felt something strange. I had the head, beak, and comb and a bit of the neck all in one, awful-looking mess. The Indian brothers saw what happened and gave me part of a spicy breast. One of them remarked, "They don't waste any part of the chicken; it's a delicacy."

What wore me down the most, however, was the constant, daily exposure to the Indian masses. People were everywhere. Many years later when N. J. Varughese came to America for the first time he asked me as we drove across the country, "Where are all the people?" In India the streets are packed with humans walking in droves. He was astonished that all he saw was cars, other vehicles, and more cars.

In India I found it nearly impossible to be alone. Inquisitive onlookers would incessantly peep in the windows. The children would often cry when they saw me. Some ran away in fear. I was the first white man they had ever seen.

I stopped the truck at the edge of a huge *mela* — festival or open market. Thousands of people had gathered to sell or barter goods in a carnival-like atmosphere spread over a few acres. I sat behind the steering wheel as the team began to sing at the rear of the truck. A curious crowd gathered to see what we had in the boxes.

"Books! Good books for sale. Good News books!" The brothers shouted as they hurriedly grabbed the precious cargo and began handing samples to potential buyers. We had learned to take advantage of frenzied buying. It was sort of a crowd instinct causing them to think that if they did not purchase the Good News quickly they might lose the chance.

Our books and Bibles were subsidized so the price was reasonable for a villager. Gospel tracts were freely distributed everywhere even along the road as we drove by people and through villages. The price of the books, however, was weighty enough that the literature was valued and not considered propaganda. On the other hand, the communists were freely giving literature in their attempt to gain followers. We heard many people say "propaganda", thinking we were communists until they realized the books were for sale. It was a great joy to see tens of thousands enthusiastically purchasing the Word of God. Only the Lord knows the result of all that Word distributed throughout India.

I could not move myself from the cab to the rear of the truck. I was emotionally exhausted. *Was I having a nervous breakdown? How could I face all these people again?* Demoralizing thoughts filled my mind.

This time nothing seemed to spark the sale. People were standing around looking at each other. The team sang another song in an attempt to ignite a buying spree but again it fell flat. Chacko came looking for me. When he opened the door, my distress was evident. He smiled kindly and said, "Just rest awhile." It was reassuring that he had not judged me or made me feel guilty.

After a few more minutes I managed to pull myself up. Completely against my feelings I hopped out and went to the back of the truck. I grabbed a large stack of Gospel packets and began shouting at the top of my lungs. *"Sousamachar, Sousamachar. Jesu Mashi kai Jiwan"*, I yelled, meaning "Good News, Good News. The life of Jesus Christ."

Our Gospel packets were large sandwich bags with two Gospels, usually John and Mark, and a Bible correspondence course application all in the local language. My voice sparked the sell. A buying frenzy erupted. Soon my pockets were once again bulging with Indian rupees. What a joy it was to see children walking away reading the Word of God to others around them. Though many do not read in India, we knew that in every village there were some who would read to the illiterate.

I had no strength or desire to get out of that cab. Where had it come from? Is this what Jesus meant in Luke 9:23 when he said deny yourself and take up your cross daily and follow him? Is this what the Apostle Paul wrote about when he was in the Philippian jail cell?

> *I know what it is to be in need, and I know what it is to have plenty. I have learned the secret of being content in any and every situation, whether well fed or hungry, whether living in plenty or in want. I can do everything through Him who gives me strength* (Philippians 4:12-13 NIV).

Though I had no strength or emotional energy, I had exercised my will in obedience to His command to "go into the whole world." God did not shove me out the door. I had to choose obedience in order to experience

His life and victory. God was teaching me the difference between living according to my feelings and living by insight empowered by the Spirit of God. That is a *mother lode* lesson.

Village life was simple but hard. The women would search the forest for sticks and tree limbs and then carry them bundled and balanced on top of their head. We often saw them walking alongside the road with a certain rhythmic sway that belied the heaviness of their burden.

The young boys and girls followed the sheep, goats, and cattle around the fields as they foraged for anything green and edible. The cow dung was collected in baskets and hauled back to the village. It was hand mixed with straw and clapped into patties that were then stuck on the side of mud huts. When dried they were used with the wood to stoke the clay ovens for cooking. These chips were clean-burning and odorless. The cow dung mixed with water also was used to create a polished smooth floor in the thatched houses. These dung floors lasted about one year before they had to be redone. We rolled our sleeping bags out on many such floors and slept comfortably. I could never detect any odor.

Water or the lack of it was a major problem in many places. The ponds, called tanks, in the villages were used for all purposes. At one end you could see water buffalo lying down nearly submerged and being hand washed by their Indian cowboy. On the opposite side women were beating their clothes on a flat stone propped up at waters edge alternately rubbing them with a bar of soap and swishing water over them. It was the local laundromat. Closer to the village you could see ladies filling their metal or clay pots for drinking and cooking purposes while children splashed and frolicked with their friends. A good distance away other people squatted and washed themselves, flipping water on their bottoms with their left hands after defecating.

One craving I had in those remote villages was for a glass of pure, cold, drinking water. They had a clay pot with a long neck which was called a *sarai*. When placed in the shade and exposed to the wind or draft in the house, it kept the water semi cool. It was the closest thing to a cold water drinking fountain I was able to find. In one rural area we were so thirsty as the midday, tropical sun beat on our heads, that we gladly received a glass of water from a farmer's well. It looked crystal clear as I tipped it down my dry throat. With just an inch or so left at the bottom of the glass, I noticed some movement. Holding it up to the blistering sunlight, I saw what looked like miniature maggots squiggling around in what would have been my last gulp.

On another occasion as we were eating seated on the mud floor of a hut, a black scorpion the size of a small lobster crawled across the ground just a few feet from me. I don't think I budged but simply made a comment and kept eating. Later one of our brothers accidentally stepped on a poisonous snake. He was not bitten. But the snake was killed. Jesus said to the seventy disciples that he sent out,

> *I saw Satan fall like lightning from heaven. I give you the authority to trample on snakes and scorpions and to overcome all the power of the enemy; nothing will harm you. However, do not rejoice that the spirits submit to you, but rejoice that your names are written in heaven* (Luke 10:18-20 NIV).

He also told them to,

> *Go into all the world and preach the gospel to every creature. He who believes and is baptized will be saved; but he who does not believe will be condemned. And these signs will follow those who believe; in My name they will cast out demons; they will speak with new tongues; they will take up serpents; and if they drink anything deadly, it will by no means hurt them; they will lay hands on the sick, and they will recover.* (Mark 16:15-18)

Many Christians whimsically follow signs, but Jesus said that signs would follow them. Somewhere following the Spirit-empowered believer are miracles!

I did not knowingly drink that contaminated water nor did our brother deliberately step on the viper, but I believe that God protected us from those and many other possible tragedies as we followed his commandments. As for Satan falling like lightning from heaven, we cast demonic spirits out of an old village woman who was leaping like a wild panther. Her face, obviously not her normal countenance, was contorted as she angrily growled at us. She was delivered and later became a stalwart believer in that village where we planted a church.

Headlines in the newspaper the next week reported a meteorite falling to the earth in the same vicinity where we dealt with the old woman. I clipped it out and included it in my monthly newsletter. Coincidence? What are the odds of a meteorite falling from the night sky in the same vicinity at about the same time where we cast out demons? I chose to believe that it was God smiling on us and chuckling as He arranged for the meteorite from deep space to fall so close to our confrontation with evil. What Jesus saw in the spirit, *Satan falling like lightning from the sky*, our Father orchestrated in the natural realm for us.

Superstition and spiritual darkness are stifling and deeply rooted in the Indian psyche. Jay Prakash our high caste, Brahmin-convert, as a new Christian discovered that the meat he had eaten a week earlier was beef and not goat. His old superstition caused such repulsion that he vomited. I saw people bowing down to worship a full moon, Hindu holy men drinking cow urine to purify their souls, and worshipers gargling the putrid waters of the sacred Ganges River beside the cremation platforms as they bathed, hoping against hope to wash away their sins. India was so different than what I was used to. I felt like my mind was having cramps.

My first year in India was a super cultural shock. I was ready for a break in the routine. We all were. The OM leadership had arranged for a conference in Katmandu, Nepal. All of the north Indian teams converged on the capital of the only country officially declared as a Hindu nation. Even India did not have that distinction.

No one knew, but I had decided to leave India after the conference. As a team we had been through lots of trials and faith-stretching experiences. We had bonded. My understanding of the Word of God had taken on a depth and dimension that seminary could never have produced. Though we had regular studies in the Word over that year, the greatest lessons were learned by experiencing the Living Word in a foreign culture. Still I had had enough. I longed to return to familiar territory. No one was holding me though it was generally understood to be a two-year commitment. I had not signed a contract.

George Verwer, co-founder of Operation Mobilization, came to the Katmandu conference. It was the closest he could get to his beloved India. A few years earlier he had been placed on the black list. Indian immigration would not allow him entry. George always emphasized being a true disciple for the Lord Jesus rather than a chocolate soldier which melts in the heat. He was like the Apostle Paul. Wherever he preached, there was either a riot or revival.

One evening we walked together along a footpath in the hills. Katmandu lies in a valley surrounded by hills that rise in the distance to the snow-capped Himalayan Range. It was exhilarating to be there so near the top of the world. I had even gotten a glimpse of Mount Everest as billowy clouds marched across the far horizon and skipped a step to reveal its majestic face.

When I told George that I was serious about leaving India, he was quiet. Then came his firm and measured response, "Terry, I think it takes a greater call to leave India once you are here than to come in the first place!" I had no rebuttal. His words struck me as true. They penetrated my spirit. Over the next week I pondered what George had said.

Though Nepal was an avowed Hindu nation, my attention was drawn to another kind of temple. Flags flew atop a spiral dome. It was a Tibetan holy place. The Chinese had taken over Tibet in 1951. Thousands of refugees had fled across the border into Nepal and India. The Dalai Lama, revered as the reincarnation of Buddha, found asylum in India's far north.

The Tibetans are a colorful people and peace loving. Like the Hindus they were quite superstitious. The flags on the temples were for prayer. The more the wind whipped them the greater the prayer force. Older Tibetan women in their multicolored wraps twirled a spindled wheel-like canister. It was intended to generate prayers with every rotation.

The Muslims we saw had their own similar tradition. They could be seen continuously rotating beads on a hand-held necklace. Five times a day you heard loud speakers blare the mournful Imam's voice exhorting the faithful to pray. "Allah calls. It is better to pray than to eat." I saw many Muslim men who had died their hair and beard red to show that they had made the holy Haj to Mecca. (Tradition says that Mohammad had red hair.) This pilgrimage is one of the five pillars of Islamic belief. During the summer of 2006 it was headline news that three hundred and fifty-four pilgrims were trampled to death in a stampede there. Ironically it was part of a ritual in which the participants symbolically stoned Satan. In one sect of Islam I have seen participants flagellate themselves until blood runs in streams down their backs. This they do in remembrance of their ancient leader, Muhammad's nephew, Ali. This group, the Shites, forms one of the main sects of Islam. Much of the terrorism and bombings in present-day Iraq is between this group and the Sunni sect.

My dear friend, Stephen, carried Tibetan Gospels to the refugees in his area around Bangalore. His burden and love for these indigenous people grew and he dreamed of meeting the Dalai Lama and his monks. The dream became a reality when the Dalai Lama graciously received him, accepted a Tibetan Bible, and allowed him to present the message of Jesus to the young novitiates. My heart truly was saddened when I saw him on a television interview recently. With his warm and childlike grin he said that Christians had tried to persuade him to become a believer in Jesus. "That would be impossible." He chuckled. I thought, *My friend, God specializes in impossibilities.*

The Roman Emperor Constantine converted to Christ and much of Rome became Christian overnight. Persecution of the believers ceased. Of course, that is only partially true. Many did find Christ after Constantine but most served a mixture of gods and were not clearly Christian converts. The point is that God does things sometimes on a grand scale. The present move of God's Spirit in Korea is a prime example. From being a predominately Buddhist country fifty years ago, today it has the world's largest churches and a Christian population numbering well over thirty percent and growing rapidly.

Something else thought impossible occurred during this time – the Americans landed on the moon. That was the exciting news announced at our plenary session. The Nepali newspapers had photos of the lunar surface and the famous first footprint. Astronaut Neil Armstrong's humble statement, "One small step for man; one giant step for mankind" proved prophetic for me. Outer space posed an extreme challenge as the final frontier for the human race, but I was facing an extreme challenge within.

I wrestled with what George Verwer had told me. The significance of my personal decision, I concluded, was being overshadowed by a cause much greater than any one man's life and individual agenda. The Apostle Peter had proclaimed to Jesus, *You are the Christ, the Son of the living God* (Matthew 16:16 NIV). Jesus commended him for receiving that revelation from the Father. The Lord Jesus declared that was the rock on which He would build His church. It was not Peter himself. Jesus was building His church. In the verses that follow Jesus speaks to the disciples corporately. In Matthew 16:20 he warned his disciples to tell no one that He was the Christ. God has perfect timing for everything. In the next verses He explains His suffering and rebukes Peter for being a stumbling block. The Lord was giving His chosen disciples solid teaching about His kingdom which is here now but not fully. (Matthew 16:28) That is why Jesus taught us to pray *thy kingdom come, thy will be done on earth as it is in heaven* (Matthew 6:10).

The extreme adventure facing me in Nepal was what Jesus Himself described in Matthew 16:25-26,

> For whoever desires to save his life will lose it, but whoever loses his life for My sake will find it. For what profit is it to a man if he gains the whole world, and loses his own soul? Or what will a man give in exchange for his soul?'

I had been culture shocked by India and I felt that my life as I knew it was slipping away. My decision to leave was like one last gasp for air before drowning in oblivion. God called me to India as I desperately pleaded for reality in my Asbury Seminary closet. "Go to India!" He had not changed His mind, but He was changing mine. I responded to the King of the Universe. He was teaching me Kingdom principles, spiritual lessons. My schooling was not finished. George Verwer was right. I had been called to India. I had not yet been called to leave. My greatest lessons were yet to be learned. I would descend from the cool, mountainous Kingdom of Nepal into the fiery plains of Hindustan with my Indian brothers and sisters. We were building God's Kingdom together.

A few weeks later in Samastipur, India, God flooded my heart with peace that surpasses understanding. John 16:33 says,

> These things I have spoken to you, that in Me you may have peace. In the world you will have tribulation; but be of good cheer, I have overcome the world.

Philippians 4:6-7 also says,

> Be anxious for nothing, but in everything by prayer and supplication, with thanksgiving, let your requests be made known to God; and the peace of God, which surpasses all understanding, will guard your hearts and minds through Christ Jesus.

I lowered a bucket into an open well on the church compound, dipping it a couple of times to make sure it was full. A rope was tied to its handle and looped through a single pulley above the opening. I pulled the rope, lifting the bucket to the surface. With only a lungi cloth wrapped around my body and flip-flops on my feet, I slowly poured the bucket of cool water over my head.

There were no washcloths but the lathered soap and clear well water refreshingly flushed the dirt and diesel grime from my body. The Indian brothers referred to it as a "pour bath." Something very significant happened that morning. My pour bath became a rich experience. Water splashed over my head and down my body. It was like a baptism of death. My heart was singing, "It is well with my soul." I no longer live but Christ lives in me (Galatians 2:20). At that moment I felt that I could die physically in India and be happy about it.

Hebrews 6 exhorts believers to go on to maturity, to leave elementary teaching about Christ. Jesus, Himself, submitted to water baptism by John the Baptist not because he was a sinner but to fulfill all righteousness (Matthew 3:15). I was water baptized as a new believer. Now I experienced a baptism of death likened to that referred to by Jesus in Matthew 10:38-39. Predicting his death He told James and John who had asked to sit beside Him in the coming Kingdom,

> *'You do not know what you ask. Are you able to drink the cup that I am about to drink, and be baptized with the baptizm that I am baptized with?' They said to Him, 'We are able.'* (Matthew 20:22).

Furthermore the Apostle Paul exhorts us to *Set your mind on things above, not on things on the earth. For you died, and your life is hidden with Christ in God.* (Colossians 3:2-3). This is a very real experience, but it is also an on-going one. The continuing aspect is that which Paul refers to in Romans 12 NIV,

> *Therefore, I urge you, brothers, in view of God's mercy, to offer your bodies as living sacrifices, holy and pleasing to God — this is your spiritual act of worship. Do not conform any longer to the pattern of this world, but be transformed by the renewing of your mind. Then you will be able to test and approve what God's will is — his good, pleasing and perfect will."*

Dr. E. Stanley Jones wrote a book entitled *Victory Through Surrender*. The title tells exactly what the theme is, and it touched me deeply. It was such a powerful little book that Gospel for Asia, a mission organization established by Dr. K. P. Yohannan to support native missionaries and indigenous training, republished it in India. Brother K. P., with whom I worked nine years as Church Coordinator for GFA, asked me to write a brief testimonial for the cover. That book along with similar ones like Andrew Murray's *Absolute Surrender* continues to challenge Christian believers to experience the extreme adventure of abandonment to the Father and the Lord Jesus Christ.

You have heard about the man who pushed a wheel barrow across Niagara Falls on a tight wire stretched from Canada to the USA. Crowds watched intently as he slowly made his way through the mist with treacherous wind gusts nearly causing him to lose his balance at several spots. The crowd was awed. When he successfully made it to the American side, they were jubilant. He then asked the question, "Who of you believes that I can now walk across this wire to the Canadian side?" They responded enthusiastically hoping to see the feat again. "If you really believe," he shouted, "get in the wheel barrel!"

I was in my wheel barrel with Jesus and there was no turning back. My earnest hope and prayer is that if you have not already done so, you will join me in this extreme adventure.

Chapter
9

TIMES OF REFRESHING

Descending from the mountain Kingdom of Nepal I felt the favor of God on my life. We preached daily in the open markets and occasionally varied the routine by visiting hospitals and holding book expositions on college campuses. Our dialogues with Hindu students and teachers were invigorating. They shared their belief system, and in turn we shared the Gospel.

Much of the time it was hard, ground-breaking work. Most people were hearing the message of Jesus for the very first time. Some were truly ripe fruit and had dramatic encounters with the living Lord. N. J. Varughese and Joycutty formed a team of their own in south Bihar. A young Hindu college student, Satish, came to their bookstall asking questions. Varughese gave him a Scripture booklet called *Help From Above,* published by World Missionary Press in New Paris, Indiana. Satish was enraged. His father was a Hindu priest. He scolded them for propagating another religion in India.

That night in his dormitory he ripped the thin pages from the booklet and rolled *ganja* cigarettes. Instead of getting high as the smoke curled up his face, he felt deep conviction. He thought, *This is wrong. These pages speak about the One True God.* The next day he returned to the bookstall and told Varughese what happened. Satish gave his heart to the Lord right then. The change was immediate. A few years later I attended his water baptism. His whole family has become Christians including his former Hindu priest father. He is one of the Christian pastors and leaders with All India Mission founded by Brother Varughese and his wife, Ellen.

We experienced many times of refreshing as we took the message to hundreds of places like Satish's village where there had been no Christian witness. We were experiencing Acts 3:19 (NIV). *Repent, then, and turn to God, so that your sins may be wiped out, that times of refreshing may come from the Lord.* I am thankful for times like that when you are pressing on in faith being obedient to what you understand to be God's will for your life without any outward signs. Then suddenly God manifests Himself in a special way.

I am thankful for the *suddenlies* of the Christian faith illustrated in the New Testament. One hundred twenty faithful followers of Jesus Christ obediently waited for what He called the Promise of the Father. The Lord talked to them before His ascension about a baptism with the Holy Spirit *not many days from now* (Acts 1:5). Although they didn't know exactly when or what to expect, the Lord had clearly told them that when the Holy Spirit came upon them they would be empowered to *be witnesses . . . both in Jerusalem, and in all Judea and in Samaria, and to the ends of the earth* (Acts 1:8).

That happened ten days later as recorded in Acts 2:1-4. It happened in God's perfect timing – *When the Day of Pentecost had fully come* – and it happened suddenly. C. S. Lewis, the great English author and ambassador for Christ, entitled his autobiography *Surprised By Joy* because he was touched gradually then suddenly and unexpectedly with insight into the reality of truth. Dr. Jack Deere, a former professor at Dallas Theological Seminary, wrote his testimonial book with a similar title, *Surprised By The Power Of The Spirit.* He related *experiencing* biblical truths that had formerly been only cerebral.

Our team had been pressing on for weeks without much observable results. The Word was going out but it was tough plowing. The spiritual ground was hard and rocky. Opposition and suspicion were constant companions.

One morning after personal devotions, we routinely gathered for a time of worship and teaching from the Word. As I read the account of the crucifixion of Jesus in John 19, I suddenly started to cry. There was absolutely no precursor or warning of this manifestation. I was just reading the Bible which was our daily custom before distribution of literature. I was amazed and completely nonplussed by my own tears and behavior.

The Indian brothers were stunned – speechless. Weeping continued a long time. Some of the brothers bowed reverently. Others began to shed tears also. Then, just as suddenly, my weeping shifted to laughter. By this time we were all becoming excited, weeping and laughing simultaneously. I could imagine outsiders observing the scene. The natural reaction would have been much the same as on the Day of Pentecost though speaking in different languages was the recorded manifestation then. At Pentecost some were amazed, some were perplexed, and others simply dismissed it as a drunken party. We had tongues manifestation also. The brothers spoke different languages and worshipped in different languages as well as English. Some of the languages I partially recognized and others were unknown to me. They sounded strange. (Acts 2:5-13)

In reality we were all revived and refreshed. With new energy and enthusiasm we preached the Gospel and spread God's Word. Our worship together and privately was permeated with a sense of awe, a holy fear, and expectancy (Acts 2:43) ordered by God rather than the cut and dry order of man. It was more like what I read about in the New Testament Church.

> *And when they had prayed, the place where they were assembled together was shaken; and they were all filled with the Holy Spirit, and they spoke the word of God with boldness* (Acts 4:31).

It was a tremendous confirmation to us that we were not alone. We were fired up (Matthew 3:11) and preached more boldly after that.

Jesus taught much about the Holy Spirit. In John 14:18 (NIV) He said, '*I will not leave you as orphans; I will come to you.*' We were not alone in this extreme adventure. It was not a mind game in which we were trying to convince non-Christians to believe in Jesus Christ. The Holy Spirit really was working in us and through us as we followed His commandment to go to the whole world with the Gospel.

He was with us in reality not just in our thoughts. Jesus called the Holy Spirit the Comforter or the Helper (in the Greek literally: One who goes alongside) '*whom the Father will send in My name, He will teach you all things, and bring to your remembrance all things that I said to you*' (John 14:26). In John 16 Jesus teaches that it was best for the disciples that He go so the Helper would come.

So the Holy Spirit was sent by both the Father and the Son to dwell within us and to empower us. (John 16:7 and Acts 1:8) The unexpected refreshing we experienced was God's way of showing us that this was His business. It was His will that these people hear the message and respond.

In John 7:17 (NIV) Jesus said, *If anyone chooses to do God's will, he will find out whether my teaching comes from God or whether I speak on my own.* That is a very potent statement and our OM team found out by experience.

Was it truly God's will that we preach the Good News in India?

Jesus had only the Old Testament revelation. He knew the prophecy of Joel 2:28-32.

> *And it shall come to pass afterward that I will pour out My Spirit on all flesh; your sons and your daughters shall prophecy, your old men shall dream dreams, your young men shall see visions. And also on My menservants and My maidservants I will pour out My Spirit in those days. And I will show wonders in the heavens and in the earth: blood and fire and pillars of smoke. The sun shall be turned into darkness and the moon into blood, before the coming of the great and awesome day of the LORD. And it shall come to pass that whoever calls on the name of the LORD shall be saved. For in Mount Zion and in Jerusalem there shall be deliverance, as the LORD has said, among the remnant whom the LORD calls.*

In seminary we studied about the Holy Spirit. It was listed in the academic syllabus as *pneumatology,* Study of the Spirit. In India we experienced the Holy Spirit and this experience confirmed for me that the Bible is trustworthy in what is recorded in the book of Acts. Certainly the Bible is true whether we experience it or not.

Peter defended what happened in the upper room by quoting this same passage from Joel. *These men are not drunk, as you suppose. It's only nine in the morning* (Acts 2:14-21 NIV). The One whom we were experiencing was not an it, force, or spiritual influence. He was and is God.

The unexpected outpouring we experienced made a big difference in the atmosphere of our team. The singing was livelier with lots of joy. We felt uplifted. It was a high. Prior to my conversion I had experienced the high of being intoxicated and the high of narcotics prescribed temporarily for pain by my doctor. Those worldly feelings of euphoria left me empty inside with no lasting peace of mind. There was no joy and no sense of being righteous, only hangovers and crashes. The uplifting that we experienced as a team was what Paul described in Romans 14:17 as the Kingdom of God. F*or the kingdom of God is not eating and drinking, but righteousness and peace and joy in the Holy Spirit.* It is the Kingdom – His ruling which Jesus said was *within you* (Luke 17:21).

The world offers poor counterfeits that are not worthy to be compared to the uplifting God has for believers. Tragically many have settled for imitations. My sincere hope and earnest prayer is that this writing will stir young people to embrace the extreme adventure of Jesus Christ and experience the abundant life for themselves (John 10:10). Many are risking their lives for much lesser things. I saw three young men engulfed in flames. They were burned alive in their car because of impetuous foolishness, the thrill of speed and racing under the mind-numbing effect of drugs. The heat was so intense that I could not help them. I had to stand there helplessly, shaking and weeping. I have ministered to a young man dying of AIDS. Sex had been his god. I stood by unable to offer any help whatsoever except the words of Jesus.

People readily take risks. Why not take the risk of faith in Jesus Christ? Psalm 34:8 says, *Taste and see that the Lord is good.* God and His Word are completely reliable.

Another result of our unanticipated spiritual visitation was thankfulness. We felt so very blessed. Our cup was running over. All the world has to offer can never satisfy the deepest longings of the human soul. Dissatisfaction and disappointment are the chief signs of this age and generation. Restlessness and emptiness prevail; artificial adventures have been created to fill the void. Reality television programs are symptomatic of the American culture especially where boredom reigns. These shows are far from reality.

God has used television greatly but so has the devil. It is church for many true shut-ins, but it is no substitute for Body life in Christ. Our team-life afforded ample opportunity to learn the attitude of being thankful in all things. (Ephesians 5:15-21, Colossians 3:15-17, and 1 Thessalonians 5:18)

We had been captivated by a purpose and reality worth living and dying for. The Judeo-Christian worldview is that Almighty God created each of us with a purpose. Each one has a destiny not to be determined but to be discovered. St. Augustine said, "Our hearts are restless until we find our rest in Thee, O God." 1 John 5:12-13 says,

> *He who has the Son has life; he who does not have the Son of God does not have life. These things I have written to you who believe in the name of the Son of God, that you may know that you have eternal life, and that you may continue to believe in the name of the Son of God.*

No matter how good or bad your life is right now, without a conscious relationship with the living Christ, the Bible says you exist without life. Without Him you may laugh loud at parties or be the center of attention with your off-color jokes, but you are dead inside. Perhaps the blank stare of apathy, like a mask of death, reveals your lonely heart when you are not surrounded by your friends.

You may be an unfeigned optimist who believes that man can and will make things better without God. But as mankind continues to run out of answers and gropes in the occult and metaphysical realms, this view is less appealing and is disappearing. You may believe that truth is relative and that there are absolutely no absolutes. You may conclude if God does exist, He is not relevant. But those are only your opinions.

Dr. Francis Schaeffer's writings over thirty years ago predicted our present condition and this mind-set. We are living in a time when "propositional truth" (absolute truth revealed by God to man) has been replaced by opinions and human reasoning. Dr. Schaeffer proposed that society as we know it would not be able to stand. More recently, Chuck Colson's book, *How Now Shall We Live* – a title similar to Dr. Schaeffer's – confirms my conviction that following the Lord Jesus Christ is the most extreme adventure possible to man. Colson's conclusion after carefully examining all other world-views is that "only the Christian worldview provides a rationally sustainable way to understand the universe."

The times of refreshing came upon us, I believe, because we were walking in faith and quick to repent (turn) from our sin rather than dabble in it or hold unforgiveness in our hearts against each other. We were emotionally lifted, but there is something much deeper than emotion in what we experienced. We were not depending on the emotional highs to energize us for Gospel work. The times of refreshing were bonuses God sent from time to time to bless us as we obeyed Him.

> *But seek first the kingdom of God and His righteousness, and all these things shall be added to you* (Matthew 6:33).
>
> *If we say that we have fellowship with Him, and walk in darkness, we lie and do not practice the truth. But if we walk in the light as He is in the light, we have fellowship with one another, and the blood of Jesus Christ His Son cleanses us from all sin. If we say that we have no sin, we deceive ourselves, and the truth is not in us. If we confess our sins, He is faithful and just to forgive us our sins and to cleanse us from all unrighteousness.* (1 John 1:6-9).

In retrospect, I believe that in those early days in India our 'walking in the light as He is in the light' with each other created the atmosphere for our unity. We were of one heart and one soul with no one having much more than anyone else. God's grace was upon us as we gave witness with great power. (See Acts 4:32-33.)

A. Stephen was working with another team at this time in Uttar Pradesh which has the highest population of any state in India. His team had experienced some disunity. With such diverse backgrounds it is understandable that disagreements might happen, especially living in such close quarters. Stephen was burdened. He prayed. The same night he wandered up a cleared knoll not far from the team's camp. With the full moon glowing brightly above him he poured out his heart to the Lord.

Stephen knew five Indian languages at that time, but he did not know the local language at all. Suddenly the Holy Spirit came upon him in such a way that he began to shout. But his shouting was not in a language he recognized. At first he thought it was just a gibberish overflow of his emotional release. His voice became louder and louder. When he opened his eyes, local people were standing around staring at him. Several of the OM team members had heard the commotion and ran to see what was happening. Some of the locals were bilingual.

When they discovered that Stephen did not know their mother tongue, they were dumb-founded. He had been glorifying God in their own language. They had understood! Needless to say this unexpected miracle brought reconciliation, wonder, and revival to the team.

Though we were not depending on our emotions, the times of refreshing God poured out on us kept us from spiritual dryness. I understand feelings to be like the caboose of a train. The locomotive is the facts of the Christian message. The coal car attached to the engine is like our faith that regularly supplies the energy when shoveled into the furnace. The train could run with or without the caboose. It was nice and normal to have it, but we were going forward with God no matter what.

What was happening to me? It can only be described as a song and melody in my heart. When we were walking in unity as a team, we all sensed that song and melody. As someone told me years later, "You march to the beat of a different drummer. In other words, you walk not to the rhythm pounded out by the world system but by the very beat of God's heart for His people, the lost world and the nations."

We had tasted the sweet bubbling waters of those 'times of refreshing' and knew it was real. Every generation has its popular genre of music. The present generation has punk rock and rap among others. But the melody we were hearing in our hearts was ageless and heavenly. Jesus said,

> *If anyone is thirsty, let him come to me and drink. Whoever believes in me, as the Scripture has said, streams of living water will flow*

from within him. By this he meant the Spirit, whom those who believed in Him were later to receive. Up to that time the Spirit had not been given, since Jesus had not yet been glorified (John 7:37-39 NIV).

A group of youth and counselors gathered around a life-sized statue of the Lord Jesus at a Christian campsite. It was dark but landscape lighting illuminated the magnificent white marble sculpture. Nothing was planned as we clasped hands and encircled the monument. It was a completely spontaneous gathering. We began to sing familiar choruses. Suddenly we found ourselves singing different songs. Someone was singing *Hallelujah*. Another person sang *Praise the Lord* while still others were singing *Father, You are Wonderful.* I do not know how many different choruses, known and unknown, we were singing. Some were just saying words but the words were in rhythm with everyone else. It was not all English. I heard some unknown languages being sung as well. The astounding thing was that we were all in tune and the melody was truly heavenly.

This event provoked some controversy. It was not the ordinary hymn-sing that we were accustomed to. It was extraordinarily beautiful but also a bit frightening, other-worldly. So much so that one of the teenage girls bolted from the circle and ran away. Later one of her teenage friends told us that she had been doing some things she ought not be doing and this encounter frightened her.

One of our counselors had a master's degree in music from Indiana University. She approached me after the incident, trembling and astonished. She had joined in the singing but did not understand how it happened. "We didn't have any music sheets in front of us. How did we do that? Harmonizing and blending like that takes lots of practice." She kept repeating herself: "You just can't do that. You just can't do that."

When she finally calmed down a bit, I told her that we didn't do it. "The Holy Spirit led us," I said. 1 Corinthians 14:14-15 says,

For if I pray in a tongue, my spirit prays, but my understanding is unfruitful. What is the conclusion then? I will pray with the spirit, and I will pray also with the understanding. I will sing with the spirit, and I will also sing with the understanding.

She had not seen that verse in the Bible or at least had not experienced it.

That night some were singing with their spirit to the Lord without knowing the meaning of the unknown tongues, but others were also singing with their understanding in English.

India has about 1700 languages and dialects. Our worship would often shift from one to another. Sometimes in the flow of worship we all prayed together at the same time. An outsider listening in might hear his language but also some unfamiliar ones.

Acts 2 was certainly a miraculous event. People spoke in languages they had not labored to learn. Others heard and understood them declaring the wonders of God. There were three reactions: amazement, perplexity, and mocking or making fun. Amazement is basically an emotional reaction while perplexity is a mental response of questioning the phenomenon. Mocking was a choice to ridicule. Beyond debate is the fact that one hundred twenty souls gathered in that upper room and were baptized – immersed – in the promise of the Father. They were empowered to go and *be* witnesses. The action that followed was the birth and establishment of the Church.

The speaking in tongues I understood to be prayer to God as well as miraculous communication like what happened with Brother A. Stephen standing on the knoll. 1 Corinthians 14:2-4 explains the spiritual aspect of praying and building yourself up even if you do not know the meaning of the language you are praying. The Apostle Paul quotes an Old Testament reference to this experience in 1 Corinthians 14:21 which is Isaiah 28:11-12.

> *For with stammering lips and another tongue He will speak to his people to whom he said, 'This is the rest with which you may cause the weary to rest' and 'This is the refreshing' yet they would not hear.*

Asbury Theological Seminary was a solid evangelical, biblically conservative, graduate school. My degree from Tulsa University and my conversion testimony was sufficient to gain admission. Campus Crusade for Christ had given me the basics for understanding and sharing the Gospel in *The Four Spiritual Laws* booklet. A similar one explained the Spirit-filled life showing the difference between the natural man, the carnal man – fleshly believer – and the spiritual man (1 Corinthians 2:14-3:3).

Operation Mobilization in India had exposed me to a multitude of great Christian books. Though OM was also a theologically conservative ministry influenced in the beginning by Moody Bible Institute of Chicago, some of the writings that were introduced to me expanded my understanding of the Bible. One such book was Arthur Wallis's *Pray In The Spirit*. He thoroughly and biblically explained the significance of praying in tongues – with your spirit – as compared to praying with the mind. After reading that I could not see any reason this gift should be divisive or controversial.

One of the Indian brothers from the northeast territory of Nagaland told me about the revival that came rather suddenly and unexpectedly among the Naga tribe in the early 1950s. It was ignited when a schoolteacher confessed his sin openly. This was our experience as a team also. We had learned to walk not according to feelings but according to faith in His Word. In doing so we experienced unity and Christ-like love for one another.

I found this to be the key of experiencing times of refreshing from the presence of the Lord. Notice the context of that statement in Acts 3. God had used Peter and John, who were being obedient to the Lord, to heal a lame man at the gate of the temple where they had gone to pray. Peter then preached the death and resurrection of Jesus. He urged the listeners to accept responsibility for their part in this crucifixion, repent, and put faith in the resurrected Jesus Christ. In verse eighteen Peter referred to this momentous event as being foretold by God's prophets stating that the Christ would suffer.

The cross has become a sentimental piece of jewelry that many hang around their neck. In fact it is a symbol of a very cruel and excruciatingly painful death. There is something else astoundingly significant about the cross. It is the vertical coming down from the presence of the Lord and intersecting the horizontal realm of mankind.

God, having raised up His Servant Jesus, sent Him to bless you, in turning away every one of you from your iniquities (Acts 3:26).

I think it is revelatory that in Acts 7:54-60 as Stephen was being stoned to death, he saw the heavens opened and the Son of Man standing at the right hand of God. Other Scripture references say that he was seated at the right hand of God. I believe that our Lord Jesus stood up in heaven to receive Stephen into His presence and the presence of the Father. Verse fifty-nine says, *And they stoned Stephen as he was calling on God and saying, 'Lord Jesus, receive my spirit'* (Acts 7:59). This he prayed asking the Lord not to charge them with this sin. (Acts 7:60). He was forgiving to the end.

The Ethiopian eunuch had an encounter which totally changed his life. This came about because Philip had a *divine moment* when an angel of the Lord told him to *go toward the south along the road which goes down from Jerusalem to Gaza* (Acts 3:26). It was there the eunuch happened to be reading Isaiah 53 which is clearly a prophetic description of the suffering and victorious Messiah. The Ethiopian believed and was baptized by Philip. According to Acts 8:39

> *When they came up out of the water, the Spirit of the Lord caught Philip away, so that the eunuch saw him no more; and he went on his way rejoicing.*

Who would not be thrilled and rejoicing with a visitation like that?

I believe there is a principle in these sovereign acts of God or times of refreshing from the presence of the Lord. It is the principle of the cross of Christ. God calls us to obedience. We are not to depend on our whimsical emotions. As we walk in the light as He is in the light, from time to time God sovereignly sends a refreshing from His presence. He lets us know beyond a shadow of doubt that *He Is There and He Is Not Silent*, as Dr. Schaeffer entitled one of his books.

The principle of the cross is seen throughout the Bible. Concerning man, it trumpets the truth that God Almighty will not share His glory with any other. Abraham was tested by God to sacrifice his son of promise, Isaac (Genesis 22). The Lord wants the first place of love in our hearts. Moses was called of God to deliver His people from bondage. He was reluctant but finally obeyed when God allowed Aaron to be his voice. Paradoxically, Exodus 4:24 says, *And it came to pass on the way, at the encampment, that the Lord met him and sought to kill him.* The Lord would kill (put to death) all reluctance, resistance, vainglory and carnal striving to do His will. This is the work of the cross.

On the other hand, *He who calls you is faithful, who also will do it* (1 Thessalonians 5:24). The Greek word for refreshing has to do with resting in God and His faithfulness, of being rejuvenated by that rest. As we were ministering in India, we had positioned ourselves in a place where God could send down times of refreshing. OM emphasizes love and unity with verses like 2 Timothy 2:22-26,

> *Flee also youthful lusts; but pursue righteousness, faith, love, peace with those who call on the Lord out of a pure heart. But avoid foolish and ignorant disputes, knowing that they generate strife. And a servant of the Lord must not quarrel but be gentle to all, able to teach, patient, in humility correcting those who are in opposition, if God perhaps will grant them repentance, so that they may know the truth, and that they may come to their senses and escape the snare of the devil, having been taken captive by him to do his will.*

We heard Hebrews 4 expounded as well, *Therefore, since a promise remains of entering His rest, let us fear lest any of you seem to have come short of it* (Hebrews 4:1). Mountains today are leveled and contoured by dynamite and bulldozers making way for interstate highways. But in the spiritual world we faced the mountains of dark superstitions and evil forces of bondage. We needed His empowering and the refreshing that He promised. Truly it was all by grace just as the prophet declared in this passage, God's amazing grace.

> *This is the word of the LORD to Zerubbabel, 'Not by might nor by power, but by My Spirit', says the LORD of hosts. 'Who are you, O great mountain? Before Zerubbabel you shall become a plain! And he shall bring forth the capstone with shouts of 'Grace, grace to it!'* (Zechariah 4:6-7).

The cross reveals that it is all by God's grace. I am not a good singer at all, but the Indian brothers loved for me to bellow out at the top of my lungs in my American English one of their favorite hymns. Isaac Watts composed this in 1707, but it still inspired us in Indian villages during our devotions.

When I survey, the wondrous cross, on which the Prince of glory died,
My richest gain I count but loss and pour contempt on all my pride.

Forbid it, Lord, that I should boast, save in the death of Christ my God;
All the vain things that charm me most, I sacrifice them to his blood.

See, from his head, his hands, his feet, sorrow and love flow mingled down;
Did e'er such love and sorrow meet, or thorns compose so rich a crown.

Were the whole realm of nature mine, that were a present far too small;
Love so amazing so divine, demands my soul, my life, my all. Amen.

COCONUT COBRA

In India and Sri Lanka the coconut is harvested and used regularly in preparing food. After the husk is removed the hard outer shell is broken and the white meat inside is used to cook spicy, mouth-watering curries.

One day many years after those first experiences in India, my wife, Pattie, saw what appeared to be a cobra's head sticking up in our garden next to the garage. I took a shovel and cautiously made my way to investigate. Our neighbor had recently killed a large cobra in their rice field and we certainly did not want one around our home.

As I slowly approached the suspected, slithery, intruding serpent with shovel in hand, it became clear that it was not a cobra after all. Instead it was part of a cracked coconut shell stuck on top of a stick. As Pattie and some friends huddled together at the door staring out at me, I flailed away as if beating the cobra over the head and yelling frantically as though I were in a life and death struggle. They were aghast. Then I quickly reached down and picked up the broken shell and said: "It's a coconut cobra!" After a squeamish sigh of relief we all had a big laugh.

The cobra is part of the Hindu pantheon. In one city we came upon a roundabout in the road, a circle with streets branching off in different directions. In the grassy center was a huge statue of a god with a cobra wrapped around it. The snake's flat head was menacingly suspended above the god. I asked one of the brothers who had been a Hindu why the cobra was so honored. "Fear," he said. There is ample reason to fear a live cobra.

In the Genesis account of the serpent and Eve, there was no fear attributed to man until they disobeyed God. Of course there is a positive aspect of fear. Toddlers must learn fear of a hot burner. Likewise there is the fear of death or hell. Fear is a valid level of human response.

Jesus taught that we should fear God rather than man (Matthew 10:27-31). But the fear of God that He taught was an extreme reverence. This fear of God brings peace, reconcilliation, forgiveness, and wholeness to the believer. The Cobra and other Hindu gods foster fear in the worshippers without assurance or inner peace. That is why the Indian believers love Jesus so much. He is their Savior. In love He shed His blood and died for them. God raised him from the grave, and He lives to make intercession for all who trust Him. Romans 5:1 says,

> *Therefore,having been justified by faith, we have peace with God through our Lord Jesus Christ.*

The fear our brothers experienced with the other gods brought torment and continual appeasement. A favorite passage they often quoted was 1 John 4:17-19,

> *Love has been perfected among us in this: that we may have boldness in the day of judgment; because as He is, so are we in this world. There is no fear in love: but perfect love casts out fear, because fear involves torment. But he who fears has not been made perfect in love. We love Him because He first loved us.*

Our former Hindu brothers profoundly impacted us with their testimonies. God had called them *out of darkness into His wonderful light* (1 Peter 2:9). I had been raised in a Christianized country. God had to teach me spiritual reality in a country oppressed with an ironclad caste system originating in a religion of fear and superstition. According to the Hindu and Buddhist doctrine of *karma,* the effects of their previous life determines a person's present status in life. For example, a blind man or a leper suffers because he was a bad sinner in his previous life. If he is good enough in this life, he might move up in the next life to a better condition or even a higher cast; if not, he could be reborn as one of the mangy dogs that scrounge for anything edible throughout the sub-continent. People who worshipped idols and allowed human sacrifices on occasion surrounded the writers of the New Testament. Roman gladiators were like sacrifices. The spilling of human blood was applauded. In our modern thinking we often sanitize these idolatrous religions. Face to face with them in India, however, we felt the forces operating behind the belief systems. In Bihar I saw the ancient post and altar on which human sacrifices were made less than a hundred years ago. I am not surprised even today when I hear of a human sacrifice in some dark corner of India.

The Apostle Paul exhorted the Christian believers in Ephesus,

Finally, be strong in the Lord and in his mighty power. Put on the full armor of God so that you can take your stand against the devil's schemes. For our struggle is not against flesh and blood, but against the rulers, against the authorities, against the powers of this dark world and against the spiritual forces of evil in the heavenly realms (Ephesians 6:10-12 NIV).

I parked the truck in front of a *go-down* – an Indian storage facility – where our supply of Gospel packets and other literature was stocked. Rudy and I lifted a large wooden case onto the tailgate when an eerie sound came from somewhere along the road. It was a trumpet blaring from the nearby Hindu temple. Worshipers were filing out and walking down the road past the truck.

As I bent down to pick up a Gospel packet, my eyes were level to the truck bed. I could see to the other side of the road. There an Indian man dressed in the traditional white Punjabi attire lay groveling on the dusty ground. I quickly skirted around to see more clearly what was happening. The man's eyes were rolled back in their sockets, and he was foaming from the mouth. His friend stood by hopelessly staring, not knowing what to do. I thought, *This must be an epileptic seizure.* I had seen them before. Deep within me, however, I had an impression to pray for the man. Kneeling beside him I prayed quietly but firmly, "In the name of Jesus come out!" I had no idea how to pray specifically for this stranger, so I found myself praying in a language of my spirit – an unknown tongue. Immediately the man's countenance began to change. He quickly came out of the seizure, stood up, brushed off his baggy trousers, and proceeded down the road.

We had studied *angelology* in seminary, and it included the study of fallen angels and demons. But India exposed me to the reality of the spirit world. I was becoming increasingly aware of a difference between my rational thinking and impressions in my spirit. Though it was not always apparent, there were times that my mind and my spirit did not agree.

Jesus breathed on His disciples and said, *Receive the Holy Spirit* (John 20:22). I think his breathing on the disciples was for a grand purpose. It was not to give them goose bumps. It was not for them just to feel the closeness of the resurrected Lord. It was for them to take in His breath – His Spirit. That is real closeness! Jesus explains further this intimacy with the words, *On that day* (Pentecost) *you will realize that I am in my Father, and you are in me, and I am in you* (John 14:20 NIV).

My mind said, *It's just a coincidence that his countenance began to change the moment I prayed in the name of Jesus with my spirit.*

Our minds tend to rationalize situations. My spirit, on the other hand, received the Word of God and prompted me to act in obedience to it. Paul describes what was happening in me.

> *For the Spirit searches all things, yes, the deep things of God. For what man knows the things of a man except the spirit of the man which is in him? Even so no one knows the things of God except the Spirit of God. Now we have received, not the spirit of the world, but the Spirit who is from God, that we might know the things that have been freely given to us by God. These things we also speak, not in words which man's wisdom teaches but which the Holy Spirit teaches, comparing spiritual things with spiritual* (1 Corinthians 2:10b-13).

Some states in India have passed anti-conversion laws. Specifically these laws are aimed to restrict the growth of Christianity. Multiplied thousands of tribal people are now believers. Hindus are also turning to Christ in great numbers. On my first arrival in 1968 there were few churches in the north. Now churches are in almost every major town and city. Even village churches have sprung up all over the countryside. The Indian government will not print the actual statistics because the growth of the Christian population might cause a national uproar.

At the same time there is a reactionary movement of fanatic Hinduism. Our team was held at a local police station for no other reason than we were preaching the Gospel. We were living the Book of Acts. You read about the apostles being jailed and warned not to teach about Jesus (Acts 5:18-29). They replied, *We must obey God rather than men!* We also were endeavoring to obey God by being sensitive to what the Spirit was saying.

A young lady asked our team to pray for her. Though she was a baptized Christian, she was reared in an idol worshipping family. She attended church regularly now, but sometimes she would *go off* during the service, gyrating, swaying, and causing quite a disruption. She had been prayed for, but the problem persisted. Two older sisters in the Lord were very concerned and brought her to our prayer meeting. She joined in the worship and appeared normal until we began singing about the blood of Jesus and praying. At that time she started to manifest abnormal behavior. When I lifted up my head, the young lady was growling like a mad dog. Her hands were extended toward my neck as if she wanted to choke me. I remember her eyes were as wide as a heifer's, filled with hate. This normally demure young woman wanted to kill me!

Instead of reacting to her, a love and compassion – not my own – welled up in my heart. Scripture began to flow into my mind. "Do you understand me?" I questioned her face to face. She managed to nod her head affirmatively but kept growling. Jesus asked the Gadarene demoniac what his name was (Mark 5:9). He wanted a response, and so did I.

"God knew you before you were formed in your mother's womb," I said. (Psalm 139:15) I did not cite the references, but the Word rolled out of my mouth. It was coming from my spirit to my mind. I had not planned to speak the Word. It just happened. Perhaps it was the Word that I had hidden in my heart over the years. Amazingly her countenance seemed to change with every word I spoke. I was like a surgeon skillfully using a scalpel to cut away evil, completely unrehearsed. The Word of God sprang from my innermost being like streams of living water (John 7:38). It was an alive Word,

> sharper than any double-edged sword, piercing even to division
> of soul and spirit, and of joints and marrow, and is a discerner of
> the thoughts and intents of the heart (Hebrews 4:12).

I saw that Scripture like I had never seen it before. Spirit and soul are two different parts of the person. How much of her behavior was actually a spiritual problem and how much was just of the flesh – emotion and psychological – I don't know.

"When you were in your mother's womb," I told her, "you had no choice. Your mother took you into the temples. She ate the food sacrificed to the gods. You felt the fear that she felt. But listen to me. In the womb you started to move on your own. You stretched. You kicked. You were exercising your God-given will. Now I want you to do the same thing with your spirit." The Bible says,

> There is no fear in love. But perfect love drives out fear, because
> fear has to do with punishment (torment) (1 John 4:18).

Fear had been her problem all along. God had revealed it to me as we ministered to her. (The team was praying while I was speaking the Word.) Fear would come on her suddenly even during worship services. She did not know how to handle it. She was actually afraid of having those fears come on her.

Her sudden and unreasonable fears led to panic attacks. They were frequent enough that she sort of expected them to show up. When they did, she gave into them and thus lost control of her body.

While I was ministering to her, the Holy Spirit brought James 4:7 to my mind and I quoted it to her. *Therefore submit to God. Resist the devil and he will flee from you.* I told her to exercise that same will which she began to show in the womb. I urged her to now say no to the devil. She did that and experienced deliverance. She is normal to this day and serving the Lord in peace and victory.

Do I think she was demon possessed? No. She was a Christian and the Holy Spirit was dwelling within her, but she certainly had some issues – generational in this case – that were causing her serious, persistent problems.

Years later I experienced sudden terror not unlike this. We were sleeping in a second floor motel room in Austin, Texas, when a great commotion and noise jarred us from sleep. A man from two rooms away was standing somewhere on the walkway outside screaming. I pulled back the thick curtain just enough to peer outside. Unfortunately he was right in front of me on the other side of the window! Unbelievably he thrust his hand at me right through the glass pane. Blood-splattered slivers of glass sprayed my face, neck, and chest. From the scratches on my body I could not distinguish his blood from mine.

Later the police apprehended him. He had been on a bad drug trip. When I showed the policeman my scratches he said, "I'd get an HIV test if I were you." For months I experienced panic attacks when thoughts came to me that I had AIDS. I had to battle my way back to normal thinking, standing on and claiming the promises of God. I never took the test. That was ten years ago.

We read in Matthew 4:24 that Jesus'

> *fame spread throughout Syria; and they brought to Him all sick people who were afflicted with various diseases and torments, and those who were demon-possessed, epileptics, and paralytics; and He healed them.*

The Greek word for demon-possessed is *diamonizomai* and is more correctly rendered 'demonized.'

Satan is referred to as the god of this age who blinds people from the light of the Gospel (2 Corinthians 4:4), and he knows that his time is short on the earth in the light of eternity. Therefore he is full of rage (Revelation 12:12). Because God has given His children the mandate to carry the Good News to all people before the end of all things, it is easy to imagine that Satan and his fallen angels would target Christians, especially pioneer church planters and those helping them.

The Apostle Peter is an example of a man of God who was demon oppressed. He could not bear to think of Jesus suffering and dying, and so he was demon oppressed – Satan messed with his mind. He had wrong thinking (Matthew 16:15-23). He loved the Lord Jesus and received the revelation that Jesus was the Christ, but soon thereafter he was rebuked by the Lord who commanded, *Get behind me Satan!*

Living in India and Sri Lanka for a composite of over nine years expanded my understanding of the spiritual aspect of life. I discovered that the suicide rate in Sri Lanka is the highest per capita in the world. There is a pervading sense of hopelessness which is evident at Buddhist funerals. On the anniversary of a loved one's death Buddhist monks offer mournful chants throughout the night. We often read newspaper reports of people taking poison for what seemed to be trivial matters. One man took poison when his wife did not serve him tea at the normal time. A teenage romance did not work out and the couple jumped into the sea from a high cliff. That spot became known as Lover's Leap. They were not the only ones. A police watch was eventually posted nearby to discourage any further attempts. To the ordinary tourist life might seem idyllic there in Sri Lanka, but we knew differently.

One of our close friends in Sri Lanka was a converted Buddhist who is now a Christian pastor. When we first met he confided in us about his struggle with depression and thoughts of suicide. He admitted that two of his own Buddhist sisters had ended their lives. As we listened to him pour out his heart, we felt sure that we could help. We prayed with the family right then. He was the founding pastor of a church in a town along the main highway. It was a very strong Buddhist area. The atmosphere was noticeably oppressive. I understood why he might feel constant depression there. In spite of the surrounding hostility, he and his wife persevered. They built a beautiful cinder block church on a hill overlooking the town which accommodates about one hundred worshipers.

When Jesus called His twelve disciples, He gave them authority to drive out evil spirits and to heal every disease and sickness (Matthew 10:1). Our prayer was fervent and full of faith for this pastor. We expected the evil harassing spirit of suicide to leave. We commanded it to go in the mighty name of Jesus. We have seen him many times since then, and he tells us that he no longer has that problem. Not only that but he has a closely-knit group of intercessors from the joyful congregation who meet regularly for prayer.

Another pastor friend told us that when he became a Christian and received water baptism, his Buddhist father became so angry with him that he bit a chunk of flesh off his shoulder. He and his wife continue to serve the Lord in a major city of Sri Lanka.

The Word of God was becoming our life-line and daily food. We were being drawn to our knees in prayer by necessity. At one point the disciples of Jesus brought him food and encouraged him to eat. Jesus said to them, *I have food to eat of which you do not know* (John 4:32). The Lord Jesus was putting His desires into our hearts and we were consumed with that which Jesus describes in the following verses:

> *My food is to do the will of Him who sent Me, and to finish His work. Do you not say, 'There are still four months and then comes the harvest'? Behold, I say to you, lift up your eyes and look at the fields, for they are already white for harvest! And he who reaps receives wages, and gathers fruit for eternal life, that both he who sows and he who reaps may rejoice together. For in this the saying is true: 'One sows and another reaps.' I sent you to reap that for which you have not labored; others have labored, and you have entered into their labors* (John 4:34-38).

We were thankful for those saints of God who had gone on before us in South Asia. They paved the way. I loved to read biographies of the men and women of God who pioneered the work of God in centuries past. Their sacrifices were inspiring beyond words.

The Spirit of God was opening up truth to us. He was helping us to understand Scripture passages we had been only slightly acquainted with and some that we were completely ignorant of. One of those precious lessons was overcoming the evil one *by the blood of the Lamb and by the word of their testimony; they did not love their lives so much as to shrink from death* (Revelation 12:11 NIV). I had been to seminary. I was not just a go-to-church-on-Sunday Christian. But I did not know some of the very basics of spiritual warfare. How many Christians are missing out on these basics? I came to know that God has so much more for us to experience if we will step out and abandon ourselves unreservedly to the Lord Jesus Christ.

The enemy is also referred to as *the serpent of old, called the Devil and Satan who deceives the whole world* (Revelation 12:9). Notice that it says his angels were cast out with him to the earth. He is also called the *accuser of our brethren, who accused them before our God day and night* (Revelation 12:10). In John 10:10 Jesus refers to him as the thief who comes to steal, kill and destroy. You may not believe there is a devil, but that does not alter the fact of his existence.

We were following the Lord Jesus Christ, committed to His plan of salvation for the nations. He, Himself, was tempted by the devil and retorted every temptation the devil enticingly spoke (Matthew 4:1-9). What did He do?

> Then Jesus said to him, "Away with you, Satan! For it is written, 'You shall worship the LORD your God, and Him only you shall serve.'" (Matthew 4:10).

Then Satan left Him and the angels came and ministered to Him.

There truly is power in the blood of Jesus to overcome the enemy. I personally experienced that by continually 'speaking the blood' for hours at a time, breaking through an oppressive dark cloud of fear and doubt. It was like escaping the earth's gravitational pull as I literally felt like I was floating in the grace of God. Perhaps this was similar to the Apostle Paul's experience when he was caught up to the third heaven.

> I know a man in Christ who fourteen years ago — whether in the body I do not know, or whether out of the body I do not know, God knows — such a one was caught up to the third heaven (2 Corinthians 12:2).

This experience equipped me to help others. I discovered that the evil spirits Jesus commissioned His disciples to cast out could not withstand the continued pleading of the blood of the Lamb. Revelation 12:11 mentions also the word of their testimony. So speaking goes along with the blood. It is not just remembering the blood of the Lamb – Christ's sacrifice on the cross – but also actually speaking to remind the enemy that Christ has authority over the believer.

One of our American prayer partners and faithful supporters was being attacked with confusion and various family pressures. He came to know the Lord Jesus when I was his pastor in the United Methodist Church. Eventually he became a very astute Bible student and teacher himself. He and his dear wife established a strong Christian home and business. All of their children are active in the church, but the enemy got a foothold in this precious man of God, and he found it difficult even to pray. He was being harassed by Satan and faced what Paul described in 2 Corinthians 2:11: *Lest Satan should take advantage of us; for we are not ignorant of his devices* (schemes). Paul also writes about the tricks and wiles of the devil in Ephesians 6:11.

Speaking on the phone with my friend it was obvious that he was depressed and under extreme attack. Right then I told him that the enemy had no right to come into his house and cause this disruption and inner pain. I encouraged him about pleading the blood of the Lamb until break-through comes and then I prayed with him. He slowly began to plead the blood. The concept was new to him. Over the next few weeks we talked frequently, and he continued to pray more fervently this way. He regained his position in the Lord and now is teaching in his church about the reality of spiritual warfare and victory.

I have read many books on this subject to gain life-saving information. The bottom line is that our Father has made provision for us to be victorious and joyful while engaged in such combat. The book that I sent my close friend to help him get back on top was Maxwell Whyte's, *The Power of the Blood*. I learned that the abundant life of Jesus is a life of being a joyful warrior, filled with God's love for all people, and being confident of ultimate victory on earth and for eternity.

There is unspeakable joy in the assurance that God is working in you at the same time He is working through you. Indeed our Father is even using the enemy to form Christ-like character in His people.

> *And we, who with unveiled faces all reflect the Lord's glory, are being transformed into His likeness with ever-increasing glory which comes from the Lord, who is the Spirit* (2 Corinthians. 3:18).

Christians can be confident that God is patiently working in them.

> *Being confident of this very thing, that He who has begun a good work in you will complete it until the day of Jesus Christ* (Philippians 1:6).

God is working through all things for the good for us (Romans 8:28). The Lord Jesus spoke to Peter,

> *Simon, Simon! Indeed, Satan has asked for you, that he may sift you as wheat. But I have prayed for you, that your faith should not fail; and when you have returned to Me, strengthen your brethren* (Luke 22:31-34).

The Lord is praying for His disciples for He knows the enemy wants to sift, shake-up or weaken them so that they will not be good examples on the earth. Naturally the enemy will do anything to discredit Christians and the Church. This Scripture reveals to us that the Lord is using Satan's temptations and evil tactics to perfect His people so that they will in turn help and strengthen their brothers and sisters.

Most of the enemy's attacks are on the mind. We found that if a believer accepts one wrong thought it can very well become Satan's stronghold in him. Other thoughts will gather around that one and will build resentment, bitterness, bad attitudes, and other corruptible things.

The Apostle Paul writes to the church in Corinth,

> For though we walk in the flesh, we do not war according to the
> flesh. For the weapons of our warfare are not carnal but mighty
> in God for pulling down of strongholds, casting down arguments
> and every high thing that exalts itself against the knowledge of
> God, bringing every thought into captivity to the obedience of
> Christ (2 Corinthians. 10:3-5).

One of our closest friends in India is Brother Divankaran whom we affectionately call Diva. He was the original leader on our Orissa team before being called to another position. Before coming to Christ he suffered great despair and took poison. Some villagers discovered him lying along a jungle road vomiting blood and reported it to the police. An OM team had witnessed to him and given him a Gospel tract earlier in the day, but he had already decided to end his life. Police found the Gospel tract in his pocket with the OM address.

With only the tract for identification the police contacted the OM office and some brothers went to the hospital immediately. Eventually Diva regained consciousness and accepted the Lord. After many years on the team he was graduated from seminary. He and his wife, Usha, now have an effective prayer and deliverance ministry in India. He knows by personal experience what it is to do battle with the enemy and win.

After my Indian OM experience, I taught several years at Lanka Bible College in Peradeniya, near Kandy, the ancient hill capital of Sri Lanka. The training and evangelistic fervor which had been instilled within me was helpful in teaching and providing practical application there. I decided to take my class to the local market in Kandy to have an evangelistic street meeting and sell Gospel packets. Most of my students were quite unsure if we could sell any Christian literature to the Buddhists. Nevertheless I took them for an open-air meeting in front of the market. We sang and testified. People stood around and listened. Then they bought the Word of God! We returned to the campus full of joy and thanksgiving.

One of my students was a quiet young man with thick, dark horn-rim glasses. He was very observant as we preached in villages and performed Gospel puppet shows from the back of our van. Lionel had been a monk in training at a Buddhist monastery. Someone gave him a Gospel tract which he read many times. Convinced that Jesus Christ was truly the Son of God he shared his conviction with the head monk. Lionel's sincerity and frankness so touched the heart of his superior that he held no animosity but kindly remarked, "Well then, I guess you have to leave this place."

Lionel was deeply burdened for his Buddhist people. He understood their philosophy and way of life. After much prayer and deliberation he sensed the Lord calling him to the hardest and most unreached Buddhist area in the whole country, southern Sri Lanka. His dedicated wife, Lahalini, accompanied him. They had one son born to them there.

Opposition was intense, but they persevered by loving the people and doing good deeds as they preached about Jesus. They regularly visited the prison. Murderers and hardened thieves got saved. Within a few years the church had grown to over one hundred believers. Some monks became jealous and vengeful. The church was bombed but not heavily damaged. Lionel and Lahalini and the believers prayed. They knew the reality of spiritual warfare. They were laying their lives down for these people and for the sake of the Gospel.

One evening before dark two men came to the church asking for Lionel. Lahalini sensed danger as she observed the men's demeanor but had no time to warn her husband. He came around the church and was immediately attacked by them, shot through the mouth, and stabbed right in front of his wife as she held their baby boy. Lionel died on the spot.

Several pastors gave eulogies of the martyred minister at the funeral but a revered senior Buddhist monk asked permission to speak a word also. His word proved to be prophetic. Addressing the Buddhists especially who had attended or were standing outside, he said, "You have cut down the tree, but the roots will grow up again and be stronger than before."

Lahalini and the congregation in south Sri Lanka stand as lights in a dark place. They who were former murderers, thieves, abusers, proud boasters, despisers of true goodness and righteousness, or just lonely, unfulfilled people are no longer slaves to sin. They are no longer missing the bulls-eye of the target without a personal relationship to the Living God. Battles may be lost and casualties may be high, but the final outcome is sure. The sacrifice of Jesus Christ has won the war between good and evil. Our Father is ultimately in control.

A few years ago I visited there and spoke to the now grown son. The church continues to thrive under Sister Lahalini's leadership, and that congregation has even planted other churches in the area.

We Christians of the West need to take the example of our Sri Lanka brothers and sisters in this church as a challenge for greater commitment. Sin must become something we hate rather than embrace or with which we compromise. John gives us all a strong word and enlightening insight.

> *He who sins* (practices sinning) *is of the devil, for the devil has sinned from the beginning. For this purpose the Son of God was manifested, that He might destroy the works of the devil* (I John 3:8).

In Sri Lanka and India the cobra is a visible part of the religious pantheon. Statues of the Buddha sitting in his meditative state are situated throughout the country. Some of those have a cobra wrapped around them with the flat head spread above the Buddha's head as if ready to strike. Some say that the cobra protected Buddha from the rain, but we surmised that it related to the fear factor of their belief system.

With all of their intellectualizing the Buddhist philosophers are obviously unable to dislodge the haunting fear of what follows death and the grave. Nor are they able to give hope for the spiritual vacuum in the Sri Lankan heart. On the other hand, they show a certain prideful attitude in using words and concepts the average man does not understand. This is the kind of knowledge the Bible refers to in 2 Timothy 3:7 as *always learning and never able to come to the knowledge of the truth.* Jesus, on the contrary, did not teach about truth. He boldly proclaimed that He was Truth (John 14:6). *I am the way, the truth, and the life. No one comes to the Father except through Me.* Then Philip, another disciple, challenged Him, *Lord, show us the Father, and it is sufficient for us* (John 14:8).

> *Jesus said to him, 'Have I been with you so long, and yet you have not known Me, Philip? He who has seen Me has seen the Father; so how can you say, 'Show us the Father'?* (John 14:8,9).

Paul cautions us in Colossians 2:8-10,

> *Beware lest anyone cheat you through philosophy and empty deceit, according to the tradition of men, according to the basic principles of the world, and not according to Christ. For in Him dwells all the fullness of the Godhead bodily; and you are complete in Him, who is the head of all principality and power.*

I found that my relationship to the Father through His Son Jesus Christ made me a complete person, and this relationship has proven to be intellectually fulfilling as well. The Apostle Paul was a very learned man in the laws of His Jewish heritage. God gave him deep insight into the nature of man and spiritual reality. His fatherly concern for the infant churches was evident. Listen to his care for them as he warns of Satan's method of attacking the mind,

But I fear, lest somehow, as the serpent deceived Eve by his craftiness, so your minds may be corrupted from the simplicity that is in Christ (2 Corinthians 11:3).

Watchman Nee who has influenced my understanding significantly wrote, "Attacking the mind is the easiest avenue for them (evil spirits or fallen angels) to accomplish their purpose. Eve's heart was sinless, and yet she received Satan's suggested thoughts. She was thus beguiled through his deception into forfeiting her reasoning and tumbled into the snare of the enemy. Let a believer accordingly be careful in his boast of possessing an honest and sincere heart, for unless he learns how to repulse the evil spirits in his mind he will continue to be tempted and deceived into losing the sovereignty of his will" *(The Spiritual Man,* volume III, page 10). How many Christians struggle and are defeated because they do not understand this principle?

Spiritually we must also protect our minds by the continual renewing of the mind (Romans 12:2) and with the assurance of a sound mind (2 Timothy 1:7). Isaiah 26:3 really confirms our Father's commitment to us if we stay focused on Him. *You will keep him in perfect peace whose mind is stayed on You, because he trusts in You.*

We found that we could be joyful in the Lord though the spiritual battles were often fierce. Ephesians 2:6 says that we believers have been raised up together, and made to sit in the heavenly places in Christ Jesus. I do not think that Jesus appeared gloomy as he faced the enemy and dealt with demonized people. Children were attracted to him so I am sure that he smiled often and laughed robustly (Mark 10:13-16). Because of the resurrection, our victory is certain. That thought in itself is enough to make you rejoice. Before the resurrection Jesus told his followers '*you will be sorrowful,*' but he continues, '*your sorrow will be turned into joy*' (John 16:20b). The latter part of verse twenty-two continues, *I will see you again and your heart will rejoice, and your joy no one will take from you.*'

We were not alone in this battle. The Father and Son had sent us the Spirit to empower us to do what He called us for. We could sing in the midst of battle like Moses and the Israelites after crossing the Red Sea.

I will sing to the LORD for He has triumphed gloriously! The horse and its rider He has thrown into the sea! The Lord is my strength and song, and He has become my salvation; He is God, and I will praise Him; my father's God, and I will exalt Him (Exodus 15:1-2).

TWO BETTER THAN ONE

Two are better than one, because they have a good return for their work: if one falls down his friend can help him up. But pity the man who falls and has no one to help him up! (Ecclesiastes 4:9-10).

I began this extreme adventure – alone!

Jesus had good reason to send His disciples out two by two. Proverbs 27:17 says, *As iron sharpens iron, so a man sharpens the countenance of his friend.* Jesus called the disciples His friends (John 15:15).

However, I found myself on this extreme adventure alone – without a help-mate, a special friend, a lover.

I was a thirty-six year-old bachelor. Many people had tried to find a match for me but nothing ever seemed to work out right. I counseled many young people while I was a single pastor to trust the Lord in this matter. I was practicing what I preached. "If you follow the Lord and be about His business God will bring someone alongside you," I reassured them. It was advice I was determined to follow myself.

I had come to the point of resignation in this matter and felt at peace. I did not want to be alone the rest of my life, but neither would I go searching. I would return to my Asian mission field a single man. Some of the brothers in India wanted to marry me off to an Indian anyway, and I was not at all opposed to that. If God put it on a brother's heart to at least introduce me, I would go for the interview.

In India the families talk and compare notes on their prospective son-in-law or daughter-in-law. Then they let the couple meet each other in a family setting where the daughter may serve tea and cookies. The couple may talk very briefly. After that if they both seem to like each other and agree, the engagement and marriage is set. The culture is such that couples are nurtured in learning to love each other. This is the traditional way marriages are arranged in India and Sri Lanka. But God had other plans for me.

Many of my Asian pastor friends have wonderful helpmates who were arranged for them, or they arranged for themselves with the help of liaisons or some friend. I have known Asian couples who did not make it or who were miserable together. Generally speaking, however, their system seems to have worked well for them. Personally, I think that system has definite advantages over the traditional Western way of dating, falling in love, and jumping in bed and testing the waters before making a commitment, a commitment which is often conditional – depending on whether one is happy, compatible, or whatever.

Since I had abandoned my life to Jesus Christ in other areas, I resolved to trust Him in this area as well. The Lord taught about fearing God as we walk this earthly life.

> *And do not fear those who kill the body but cannot kill the soul. But rather fear Him who is able to destroy both soul and body in hell. Are not two sparrows sold for a copper coin? And not one of them falls to the ground apart from your Father's will. But the very hairs of your head are all numbered. Do not fear therefore; you are of more value than many sparrows* (Matthew 10:28-31).

God knew the number of the hairs left on my head! Though I was losing them fast, I thought God must have someone for me who wouldn't mind a bald head. The American culture is drunk with its emphasis on physical beauty and the male, Hollywood-style, stud image. It is no wonder that so many marriages end in divorce. Something is not working for us. Hollywood glitz and glamour is making some rich and famous while most who adopt the deception become poor through divorce and broken relationships.

As a single pastor, I saw many marriages destroyed because one or both partners had exaggerated expectations instilled in them by the fantasies espoused by the American media. I had been close to marriage a few times but always got cold feet for one reason or another. Sexually I had my sins of the past but a conviction that sexual intercourse was only for marriage had kept me from going all the way.

According to Jesus no man can take pride in his supposed sexual purity. He who is without sin among you, let him throw a stone at her first (John 8:7). That was the Lord's statement to those who were about to stone the woman caught in adultery. He got no takers. He also said,

You have heard that it was said to those of old, 'You shall not commit adultery.' But I say to you that whoever looks at a woman to lust for her has already committed adultery with her in his heart (Matthew 5:27-28).

I knew marriage was God's plan for most people. He created them male and female, and then it says in Genesis 2:24, *Therefore a man shall leave his father and mother and be joined to his wife, and they shall become one flesh.* I felt sure that it was God's plan for me to marry. He put the desire in my heart, but I was preparing to return to Asia as a single man alone.

I had gone to sleep as writer Josh McDowell calls it, referring to God's act of putting Adam to sleep before Eve was created from him and presented to him. I also had apparent hang ups about marriage. Why was I afraid of it? I was not quite sure until a Christian friend, Bible college teacher, and counselor, Carroll Thompson, exposed them to me.

"Why can't I fall in love like any other man, and then I'll know what kind of fool I am." I confessed to Brother Carroll that I heard that song on the radio many times and identified with the character. His discerning spirit read me like a book. We did not spend countless hours in psychoanalysis and dream interpretation. Carroll is a humble man of God. He is one of the most Christ-like men I have ever known. I trusted him. He has the gift of discernment.

Unless a grain of wheat falls into the ground and dies, it remains alone (John 12:24). Brother Carroll spoke that word to me as his penetrating eyes blazed with the Lord's gentle love. As we sat at a booth in a fast food joint in Dallas, Texas, he said firmly, "You have three problems which are keeping you from marriage."

Confidently he began to lay them out, writing his points on a tablet so I could see. "First," he said, "you have an idol in your mind. You have imagined or fantasized a perfect woman to meet all your needs. This is pride. It is perfectionism. You need to repent and be open to God's choice." My spirit received his word. I knew it was true.

"The next two problems are linked together. They are fear and looming disappointment. They both are a result of pride and fantasizing. You fear that you will be disappointed, and because you are a man of covenant, you have no way of escape once you are married. You have not yet grasped the passionate love that Jesus Christ has for His Church. It is reflective of the unconditional love a husband is to have for his spouse."

I knew everything he said was right for me. As a young single pastor, I had already counseled many couples myself. As a minister, I had set a standard that I would not perform a marriage ceremony unless we had at least four counseling sessions together. I had also determined that the couple should read some helpful books. Excellent marriage preparation manuals were also available and practical when studied together as a couple.

Now it was clear that I needed some deliverance ministry in this area myself. We prayed together, and that was the beginning of gaining back the ground I had given over to the enemy through wrong thinking and fantasizing. Deuteronomy 1:8 reads,

> *See, I have set the land before you; go in and possess the land*
> *which the LORD swore to your fathers — to Abraham, Isaac, and*
> *Jacob — to give to them and their descendants after them.*

The people of God were given the land by God, but they still had to go in and do battle and take possession of it. So also we Christians must battle to regain ground that we have knowingly or unknowingly given over to the enemy. This is the land within us, our patterns of thought. Understanding this truth and the biblical truth of covenant are essential to experiencing a loving, lasting marriage.

One thing was for sure it would take a very special person to understand me and stick by me no matter what. God was revealing strongholds in my life that needed to be demolished (2 Corinthians 10:3-6). There was a war that needed to be won within me. There were broken relationships in the past that caused blind spots in the present (I John 2:11). We often do not see our own faults until they are exposed through being closely linked with another person such as a husband or wife.

Sexual counseling should definitely be part of the overall marriage counseling agenda so that any hang-ups either person might have will be exposed and healed before covenant vows are taken. Terry Wier's book, *Holy Sex, God's Purpose and Plan for Our Sexuality,* will always be a must reading for every couple I counsel in the future. 1 Peter 5:8 says,

> *Be sober, be vigilant; because your adversary the devil walks*
> *about like a roaring lion, seeking whom he may devour.*

Many are being devoured by the enemy in this area of life – sexuality and marriage. Being sober speaks of mental sharpness – of not being drunk and duped by sexual lust. Vigilant speaks of not letting your guard down – of being alert at all times. The enemy is roaring loudly with his perversion of sex and destroying many marriages. His purpose is to deaden us to the concept and reality of covenant marriage that is represented by Christ's love and care for the Church. Ephesians 5:22-33 is a very important passage of Scripture that is worthy of meditation and essential for understanding God's plan for family.

God was opening my spiritual eyes (Ephesians 1:18) with deeper truth, and it was a humbling experience – an extreme adventure. Along with the humbling, God was fortifying my heart also with more grace.

> *God resists the proud, But gives grace to the humble. Therefore humble yourselves under the mighty hand of God, that He may exalt you in due time, casting all your care upon Him, for He cares for you* (I Peter 5:5b-7).

God was preparing my heart for His wonderful gift to me. Proverbs 18:22 says,

> *He who finds a wife finds a good thing, and obtains favor from the Lord.*

Even with all this additional insight one fact remained. I was still on this extreme adventure – alone.

Don Allen, the same missionary who had influenced me to pray about Sri Lanka had spoken in a United Methodist Church in southern New Jersey. Pattie Guarini attended that meeting and responded to the altar call. God gave her a verse she had never seen before. It was John 15:16.

> *You did not choose Me, but I chose you and appointed you that you should go and bear fruit, and that your fruit should remain, that whatever you ask the Father in My name He may give you.*

She had been working for a Christian radio station but felt that God had more for her to do. At the altar the missionary counseled with her and recommended that she continue in her local church, playing the piano, and serving the Lord there. Although he recognized her need for further emotional healing from past hurts, he left the door open for her to come to Dallas as the mission's secretary if God called her there. I think what that missionary did was truly led of the Lord.

When Jesus called his disciples, he forthrightly said unto them, *Follow Me, and I will make you fishers of men* (Matthew 4:19). He didn't tell them to get their act together, to wash the smelly fish scales off their hands, to change into appropriate preaching attire, or go regularly to the synagogue to pray for one month. He said I will make you fishers of men. The door of opportunity that the missionary speaker left open to

Pattie was like a seed planted in her heart. She could not dismiss it. It germinated within her.

The Lord Jesus called the rich young ruler to come follow him. But when He told him he would have eternal life if he sold everything and gave it to the poor, the young man was really upset because he was very wealthy. Jesus did not chase after him, but this confrontation moved Peter to remark,

> *"See, we have left all and followed You." So Jesus answered and said, "Assuredly, I say to you, there is no one who has left house or brothers or sisters or father or mother or wife or children or lands, for My sake and the gospel's, who shall not receive a hundredfold now in this time — houses and brothers and sisters and mothers and children and lands, with persecutions — and in the age to come, eternal life"* (Mark 10:28-30).

Pattie was from a wonderful Polish-Italian family of ten brothers and sisters. She had never lived far away from them or her parents. They are a closely knit family. It was a daring step to pick up stakes and move two thousand miles away to a big city where she knew no one. But the call of God would not let her settle back to things as normal. Within two weeks she called the Dallas office to say she was coming. Pattie became the mission's secretary with the hope of eventually going to Sri Lanka for at least a short-term experience. I met her the day she arrived, but I left the next day for Indiana to raise missionary support for myself.

Over the next three months we talked on the phone, and she would scribble greetings on my monthly financial support reports. When I returned to the mission's office, we began praying together before starting the day's work. Our friendship grew into a deep, caring love. When she read my missionary profile, she was impressed with one statement. "His mother says that he would rather preach than eat." Our time together centered around the church, missions, praying together, cooking (experimenting with new recipes), eating together, riding our bicycles to down town Dallas late at night, and visiting senior citizens at the church high-rise retirement complex.

Not only did Pattie understand me and accept me for who I was, I felt that she sincerely loved me unconditionally and would always be there for me. At the same time my love for her looked beyond the hurts of her past to see what God wanted for her in the present. God put us together. We were helpmates for each other.

I believe God has designed covenant couples to be true friends before they are passionate lovers. We were friends! We were soon to be lovers! Pattie and I were married on June 22, 1980.

Next to God Pattie is the love of my life and the inspiration for the poem I wrote to her before we left for Sri Lanka.

Walking or' the grassy hills alone,
Waves of green and wild flowers blown,
The whispering wind commands perfectly obeyed,
Played a maestro's song and danced and swayed.
I stood silently on that sea of shaking stems
And wondered is it simply nature's whims?
Oh, no, 'tis Creator's handiwork aglow,
I know.
For there along a path already trod,
A crushed lily lies flat upon the sod.
I reached down to pluck it as my own.
Such love and compassion I had n'er shown
To any flower of the field before.
'Twas loves eternal call, "Restore, restore."
Fragile petals shaking in the breeze,
I held it tenderly and saw as only a lover sees,
The beauty and worth of a single flower in the sun,
Broken, bowed, praying, "Not my will but Thine be done."

In October of that year we moved to Sri Lanka. She had never been to Asia before or away from home that much, but she immediately fell in love with the country and the people. Truly God had prepared her heart to be a foreign missionary.

When Lanka Bible Institute was ready to make a transition to a fully accredited Bible College, the principal, Dr. Ranjit DeSilva, wanted to open the doors of evangelical theological training to all the churches on the island. Accreditation required that a certain number of faculty members have a masters degree. He knew I had been a pastor in the USA and that I was qualified. He asked me to be a part of the teaching staff in the area of Practical Theology. Pattie's secretarial ability was also needed, and her expertise would be greatly appreciated in the library. We found ourselves together on campus serving the Lord preparing ministers of the Gospel to go preach and establish churches across Sri Lanka.

Within a few months after arriving in Sri Lanka Pattie was pregnant with our first son. We were adjusting to each other after many years of single life. Pattie was immersed in a completely new culture, and we both were busy at new jobs for the Lord. All of these experiences brought great joys but also lots of adjustments. Covenant marriage is an extreme adventure in itself, but we had these added pressures as well. I thank God that we knew something about spiritual warfare and the tactics of the enemy. This established a deep unity for us as a couple. What we learned in those early years of marriage is foundational to the extreme adventure of our covenant love and marriage today.

The Song of Solomon is a wonderfully passionate portrayal of a husband with his beloved wife. It is also symbolic of the Lord Jesus Christ and His love for the Church. From the fruit of our love Nathan was born on July 28, 1981, and Timmy came on April 6, 1983. By the grace of God we also have spiritual children in Asia. We have brothers and sisters in Christ who are part of His glorious Church. They faithfully carry on the work of the Lord, and the Church of Jesus Christ is vibrantly alive and doing well.

We were not only together on the campus, but we were also together out in the market places and homes of Sri Lankan friends whom God gave us to love. We linked up with The Christian Businessmen's Fellowship and were often called on to pray for people who were paralyzed by fear. Being "helpmates" certainly means being prayer partners. Becoming united in prayer with Pattie has proven to be an extreme and wonderful adventure. We love challenges and are still learning after twenty-six years of marriage the deep joy of praying in the Spirit together.

In one Buddhist home the mother of a new born had been bound by fear since giving birth. Stones and larger rocks began to appear mysteriously in and around the house, sometimes landing on the tin roof with a shocking, sudden clatter. Rumors spread among the neighbors that the baby somehow brought a curse on the family and the house. The whole family was gripped in fear, and nothing they tried up until that time had helped.

Someone told them about our prayer team. They contacted us, and we went to their home. The young mother sat down in a chair in the middle of a small room. You could see desperation all over her face. She yearned to be free of this unnatural fear and for the stones to stop hitting the house.

As Pattie and I prayed she began to slump down in the chair. We both encouraged her to call on the name of Jesus as we shared Scriptures with her relating His great salvation. She did. Suddenly she groaned and then beamed with a beautiful smile. Sitting up straight in the chair, she asked for her baby whom she tenderly cuddled as tears trickled down her face. Later the father received Christ, attended Bible College, and now pastors a church.

We tried to be diligent in praying for safety as we traveled and for the safety of our co-workers. Psalm 4:8 says,

> *I will both lie down in peace, and sleep; For You alone, O Lord,*
> *make me dwell in safety.*

Pattie was my co-pilot in the front seat most of the time. I had to learn to drive in the British fashion, on the left side of the road. Not far from our home I came around a bend in the road and saw a tractor pulling a long wagon approaching us. Pattie saw the wagon lurching out of the lane and coming straight for us. She yelled and to this day I do not know how we missed hitting it head-on. I am sure that God's angels saved us many times.

Lanka Bible College is located in the hill country. One day as we descended a very steep hill, I heard a noise but nothing happened until we reached the bottom of the hill. Suddenly our left front wheel broke off and rolled by in front of us. Once again we were saved from near disaster. I still believe that Pattie's fervent prayers for our safety was heard by the Lord. She could be heard regularly pleading the Blood of Jesus.

When our second son was three months old, ethnic riots broke out in Sri Lanka. Thousands of people were killed, tortured, and maimed. Pattie hid three minority refugees in our house. They were being hunted down by bloodthirsty mobs in the street. Somehow an angry crowd suspected that she was harboring them, and they began to shout and demand that Pattie surrender them. She gathered some visitors together and began to pray, ignoring the shouts outside. As they prayed for safety, they also prayed for mine. I was secretly transporting refugees in our van to the refugee camps. They were lying down in the rear of the van covered with straw mats. I rounded a curve in the road and was forced to stop suddenly. A soldier stood right in front of my windshield with a carbine pointed directly at my head. I had never had a loaded gun pointed at my head before. It was tense, but we were allowed to advance unharmed. Both of these incidents happened the same day.

Now, I was experiencing my extreme adventure for Jesus with a partner. It felt so good to have Pattie at my side, one with me in purpose. Pattie and I often traveled with a Sri Lankan evangelistic team from the

Bible College. Near the Peradeniya University campus we conducted a mini crusade with a little platform and loud speaker. The crusade was near the housing where poor people lived. These were long one-story dwellings usually with dirt floors. The first night of one meeting we were drenched with a sudden downpour. The field on which we stood turned to mud but still the evangelist continued to preach the Good News of Jesus Christ. People stood under umbrellas listening to the salvation message.

Pattie and I saw something we had not seen before. The message was so powerful that some of those poor people fell down in the mud. A few started slithering like snakes. Pattie was pregnant but did not hesitate to kneel down with me in the mud as we and others on the team rebuked Satan and prayed for the release of the tormented souls. People were delivered that night and became believers. We returned to our home late, muddy but rejoicing. These were precious moments we shared together in the ministry.

God blessed me with a woman who was a soul winner and one who did not hesitate to get in the dirt and mud to see someone come to faith in her beloved Jesus. I had prayed many years before that God would give me a bold witness as a helpmate. Pattie was that person. While on a week-end holiday at one of Sri Lanka's most elevated mountain towns, she met a disillusioned Muslim woman whose husband had recently divorced her. She was ready to hear about Jesus and was moved to tears when Pattie related her personal testimony and led her in the sinner's prayer.

A year later I happened to hear a woman DJ on the radio give her testimony. It was being broadcast live from the sound studio in Colombo. She was the same young Muslim divorcee whom Pattie had led to the Lord and now she was playing hymns sung by Jim Reeves.

What we had planned as a spiritual time of refreshing in the mountains with just the two of us turned into a fruitful time of ministry. God was making us one in purpose and priority. To this day we intentionally plan weekly times of doing something special together but these occasionally turn into opportunities to serve Jesus. I am reminded of the time Jesus took His apostles aside privately into a deserted place for a time of refreshing, but the multitudes came to know about it and followed them. It was an interruption in what Jesus had planned, but consider His response.

He welcomed them and spoke to them about the kingdom of God, and healed those who needed healing (Luke 9:11 NIV).

Years before we met, God prepared my beautiful wife to be by my side when she dedicated herself to be available to God for His purposes at all times.

In this day of short term and shallow relationships, I am always greatly encouraged by those saintly couples who have learned to deny self and put the other first. They are experiencing the joy of the extreme adventure of becoming one as God originally intended from the Garden of Eden.

The enemy will do anything and everything to destroy these covenant marriages because they reflect the true glory of God's Church, the Body of Christ on the Earth. (Ephesians 5:22-33) Do not settle for anything less.

STONE AGE BROTHER

In the mid-sixties some members of our Campus Crusade for Christ Fellowship from Tulsa University along with staff leaders, Ann and Paul, drove in a caravan to visit Arrowhead Springs, California, which was Campus Crusade's main base. We attended training sessions at the headquarters, but we also took opportunities to practice what we were learning.

Someone on the headquarter staff made this penetrating statement, "If you don't value your relationship to the Lord enough to give it away, you probably won't keep it yourself." It lodged in my mind like a burr stuck on my corduroys. Naturally we wanted to share the Good News that had come to mean so much to us. We were excited about our new life in Christ, but we asked two very practical questions: "How do you share the Good News with others without offending them? How do you initiate a conversation?"

The UCLA campus was close enough for us to go there to witness. Approaching students with a survey and questionnaire on a clipboard was one method that seemed to be effective at that time.

I remember accosting a muscular young man who was sprawled out on the grassy hillside. After introducing myself I told him that we were on campus taking a religious survey. His name was Richard, and he happened to be on the UCLA football team. It was an idyllic setting. Lying there on the side of an emerald green hill on campus, sun shining brightly, I shared my faith in the Lord Jesus Christ with a complete stranger.

The conclusion of the survey led into the presentation of the Gospel. I was thrilled when Richard said he would like to receive the Lord Jesus Christ into his heart right there. We prayed together, and he invited Jesus into his life. I was fired up when we all regrouped at Hal Lindsay's apartment to share our results. Hal was the director of Campus Crusade at UCLA and later became a famous author with his book, *The Late Great Planet Earth.*

The initial objection Richard had when I finished explaining the Gospel was posed with the following questions: "What about the Stone Age people who are living in the Amazon rain forest? Will God send them to hell since they do not know anything about Jesus Christ or Christianity?" These were intriguing questions but did not prevent his praying the 'sinner's prayer' with me. I had no answer. All I could say was that God was absolutely just in all his judgments. God calls us to act justly because He is just. I recalled the Scripture that we often sang together.

> *He has shown you, O man, what is good; and what does the* LORD *require of you but to do justly, to love mercy, and to walk humbly with your God?* (Micah 6:8).

Traveling with Dr. Robert (Clem) Coleman in his car to speaking engagements, we seminarians from Asbury would often memorize Scripture together, repeating verses to each other until we had them solidly in our minds. One of those I memorized was Jeremiah 9:23-24.

> *Thus says the* LORD: *"Let not the wise man glory in his wisdom, let not the mighty man glory in his might, nor let the rich man glory in his riches; but let him who glories glory in this, That he understands and knows Me, that I am the* LORD, *exercising loving kindness, judgment, and righteousness in the earth. For in these I delight," says the* LORD.

I was assured that the Father was completely righteous in all His judgments. I had, at the same time, a compelling desire that all people, whether Stone Age or L.A. highrise dwellers – it made no difference who or where – should hear the Good News.

As I studied the New Testament, it was apparent that Jesus exuded a sense of urgency in his calling of the disciples and in thrusting them out into the world. He said,

> *I must work the works of Him who sent Me while it is day; the night is coming when no one can work* (John 9:4).

Basically He was saying that time is running out. The disciples caught this 'holy fire' and the Good News spread over the whole known world.

I did not have an answer for Richard about the Stone Age people of the Amazon jungle except that they also needed God's message and would be judged according to what light they had. My convictions about this perplexing question were eventually hammered out over the years after becoming friends with a missionary anthropologist who lived with a Stone Age tribe in the dense jungles along the Colombia-Venezuela border.

Several years later Pattie, Nathan, Timmy, and I landed at Calcutta Dum Dum International Airport. Two Christian brothers met us and arranged for our purchase of train tickets to Ranchi, Bihar. That night our stubby, yellow taxi rambled over the Hooghly River on Howrah Bridge to the station which was still bustling with travelers near midnight.

Thousands were bedding down for the night wherever we looked. Some had bedrolls, but many were just lying or sitting on the concrete platforms nearest to where their train would arrive and depart. Loud speakers announced the arrivals and departures periodically which would be followed by a chaotic rush of people, almost like a stampede.

We piled our luggage and duffle bags in a heap, sat on them, and waited. Our reserved seats and sleeping berths were located in the air conditioned car of the Bokaro Steel Express which was supposed to stop in our proximity on Platform Number 10. At least that is what the majority of Indian travelers we met had told us. Since living in India I got used to asking plenty of folks if I had need of information. You often received conflicting directions and information, so I surmised that if I asked enough people I would get a good consensus of the right information. Anyway we were fairly sure we were in the correct place.

As the train slowly chugged up the tracks to our position, people seemed to converge from every direction, scrambling for one of the doors. We were delighted that the air-conditioned coaches were reserved, and we did not have to participate in a shoving and pushing match that was typical of most Indian queues. With the help of a couple of coolies (baggage handlers who used their heads as well as their hands and arms) we found our numbered berths. The boys rolled out their sleeping bags on the top two bunks while Mom and Dad got situated below. The next morning we arrived in Ranchi. It was over one hundred degrees, but we were happy. The attendant in our car had set the air conditioner thermostat to near freezing. They had supplied us with sheets and thick, army green, woolen blankets in the night but still we shivered. We could see our breath if we dared peak out from under the covers. Upon our arrival we enquired of the porter why it was so cold throughout the night. He replied kindly that he thought since we were foreigners, we would want to be cold!

Stepping out of the air conditioned coach, the infernal heat that blasted us quickly thawed our stiff bodies. I had been to Ranchi many times, but this was my family's first experience with the real North India.

In 1975 I had returned to visit N. J. Varughese and his co-worker, Joycutty. They had left the Operation Mobilization team a few years earlier to do pioneer church planting. We had kept in touch. I always knew that God had more for us to do together. This reunion would later prove to be crucial for the birth of All India Mission in the USA.

Varughese and Joycutty were foot soldiers for the Lord in those early days after leaving OM. They took Bibles and New Testaments from the Bible Society in Ranchi on a consignment basis, packed them into their shoulder bags, and walked into the remote villages to preach the Gospel and sell enough to buy their food. If they had enough rupees, they took the bus or train as far as they could and then walked.

Unknown to me they had been praying for two bicycles. A bicycle to an Indian evangelist at that time was a prized possession. What we take for granted as a recreational toy, they esteemed as vital equipment for ministry. On that 1975 trip to the Ranchi Airport I handed Varughese enough money for two bikes, boarded the aircraft, and flew away. Months later he wrote to me saying that they had prayed two years for bicycles. God had used me to answer their prayers!

When I arrived with my family eighteen years later, the ministry had grown considerably. We saw those two bikes still in use. Now there were multiple Indian Matador vans, a jeep, and motorbikes, all being used by several teams of eager young evangelists. Most importantly we saw many churches in villages and congregations worshipping the Lord joyously and fervently. These people were really aglow with the Spirit of God.

One of our priorities for this trip was to visit the Birhor tribe. Our jeep bounced like a bucking bronco across a dusty field down a path leading to a clump of trees. Varughese had told us much about this tribe, and we were excited to finally meet some of them. They were expecting us.

The Birhor people were nomadic monkey-hunters living in tepee-like shelters that were about ten feet tall. These were constructed of sticks, tree limbs, and leaves with an oval-shaped opening at the base about three feet high. We pulled up close to a tall tree adjacent to a couple Birhor dwellings. They had prepared places for us to sit down in the shade. Before we realized what was happening a few of them knelt in front of us, removed our sandals, and began washing our feet. Pattie began to weep. It was a very emotional and humbling experience. These scantily clad jungle people known as the monkey tribe were our precious brothers and sisters in Christ. After the foot washing ceremony Nathan and Timmy curiously stooped down and crawled inside one of the tepees as goats and chickens scrambled for cover. So quickly we felt like family.

Two evangelists from All India Mission had held an open-air meeting in a village market a few years prior to our foot washing experience. Standing in the back of the crowd two teenage Birhor boys heard the Gospel for the first time. Together they raised their hands indicating they had prayed to receive the Lord Jesus. Although the evangelists recognized that the two boys were not Hindus, they were not aware of that particular jungle tribe. These teenagers were the first believers among the Birhor.

After purchasing New Testaments they returned to their clan camped deep in the jungle. Their testimony among the tribe aroused great interest and within a couple of weeks a whole clan of the Birhor walked over one hundred miles with all their belongings to the nearest church. They wanted to experience what the two boys had experienced. They wanted "Jesus to come inside them." Later, Varughese invited me to dedicate the first ethnic Bihor church.

Today there are many Birhor churches, and the tribe has made significant advancements. They now grow crops. Even the Indian government has become sympathetic and built them cinder block homes. They drive tractors and attend school. Best of all they are beloved members of a world-wide family, the Church.

Matthew 12:47-50 relates an incident in which Jesus was talking to a multitude when his mother, Mary, and his brothers showed up. One of the bystanders said to Him,

> "Look, Your mother and Your brothers are standing outside, seeking to speak with You." But He answered and said to the one who told Him, "Who is My mother and who are My brothers?" And He stretched out His hand toward His disciples and said, "Here are My mother and My brothers! For whoever does the will of My Father in heaven is My brother and sister and mother."

God has a Forever Family.

There were many other tribes in North India who added to our understanding of Jesus' grand design for His Family. Besides the Birhor believers we found Christian brothers and sisters among the Santali and Ho tribes. These happy Christians love to dance before the Lord.

On one of my visits to a remote village I had a professional photographer with me. We had to walk several miles on a winding pathway into the Indian jungle. The sound of distant drums was a friendly reminder that the tribe was expecting us. When we finally arrived, they decked us with garlands of flowers, and we danced around the center of the small village for at least a half hour. Some were dancing and beating a drum at the same time. Others were clapping bamboo sticks together as they twirled around. Some waved palm leaves. They all had broad smiles. It was a family reunion, a celebration and a taste of heaven.

Blood relation is a very strong tie throughout the world. The extended family is still the glue that holds societies together. Jesus has an extended family. Acts 20:28 says,

> *Therefore take heed to yourselves and to all the flock, among which the Holy Spirit has made you overseers, to shepherd the church of God which He purchased with His own blood.*

God's family is also a blood related family.

Sometimes natural blood-related families are broken because of a higher calling to the Family of God. Many of our Indian brothers and sisters had to leave their families for fear they would be poisoned or some mysterious accident would befall them. The Lord Jesus spoke clearly about this possibility in Matthew 10:34-37.

> *Do not think that I came to bring peace on earth. I did not come to bring peace but a sword. For I have come to 'set a man against his father, a daughter against her mother, and a daughter-in-law against her mother-in-law;' and 'a man's enemies will be those of his own household.' He who loves father or mother more than Me is not worthy of Me. And he who loves son or daughter more than Me is not worthy of Me. "*

This is an extreme adventure!

Dancing with those tribal people I felt a deep sense of awe probably like what is described in Acts 2:43. I realized then that I was part of an amazing world-wide family. This is the New Testament reality. We should expect nothing less, for Jesus Christ is the same yesterday, today and forever (Hebrews 13:8). This should not seem out of place in our present world of extremes.

Muslim young adults filled with hate are laying their lives down for a cause. They are blowing themselves up with plastic explosives in order to kill as many infidels as possible. Jesus said that this would be a sign of the end times. Nation would rise up against nation (Matthew 24:7). There are many ethnic wars in the world today.

In Sri Lanka it started with a great fury in 1983 between the ethnic majority, Singhalese, and the minority, Tamils. I was teaching my early afternoon homiletics class when the principal poked his head inside the classroom door and told me to dismiss the class and go home. At that time Pattie and I lived a short walk away from campus. Rioting had begun in Peradeniya. Our college was situated on a hill overlooking the town, and from the campus we could see black smoke billowing over the main street, drifting up toward us.

A wild-eyed mob filled with hate and revenge was burning Tamil shops on the main Colombo Road. I took my thirty-five millimeter Pentax and walked down the street snapping shots of the stores in flames. Police were standing by watching until they saw my camera. Suddenly I found myself surrounded by angry men demanding that I hand over my camera. Foolishly I had walked into the midst of a firestorm. At that moment it was too late.

Instinctively I popped open the camera and handed over the film. The enraged looters quickly dispersed and continued their dirty work. I returned to my van which was parked on the road just outside the business district. Picking up my small instamatic camera I discreetly ambled back toward the rioting, snapping quick shots along the way toward the center of town. By that time the crowd had thinned, but the damage had been done.

Soon a blood-thirsty mob marched to the Bible College entrance demanding that Tamils be turned over to them immediately. It is very difficult to distinguish between the two ethnic groups simply by appearance. I remember Brother Anton George, the college warden, standing in front of the students who had congregated outside the dining hall as the mob ranted. He was a Tamil, but speaking perfect Singhala he urged the mob to turn back. "This is a religious institution, a place of prayer, and there should be no violence here." Anton spoke confidently.

Still the main instigator pointed to a student standing behind Anton and yelled, "You, you are a Tamil!" He was actually a Singhalese student Later they got hold of the college watcher (security guard) and his nephew. They were badly beaten and hospitalized, but by the grace of God no one was killed on campus.

What truly rejoiced my heart was the unity and love I saw in the Church between both ethnic groups. I especially loved to worship with mixed congregations as we praised the Lord in both languages. Our chapel worship services were permeated with love and joy in all three languages. Among the Church family was the only place on this island nation where true love and unity between these ethnic groups could be seen. Galatians 3:26-28 speaks of the reality which we experienced during this time.

For you are all sons of God through faith in Christ Jesus. For as many of you as were baptized into Christ have put on Christ. There is neither Jew nor Greek, there is neither slave nor free, there is neither male nor female; for you are all one in Christ Jesus. .

Another aspect of our school which I loved so much was our interdenominational affiliation. Almost every flavor of Christianity was represented from Baptist to Pentecostal to Methodist and many others. One of the great benefits I saw in this was that we realized we could love each other without suspicion and still hold to our distinctive doctrinal beliefs. I was initially appointed there by the United Methodist Bishop of our North Indiana Conference. The teaching staff came from several church affiliations. Still we were truly one in Christ. I saw this as a great asset for our students. They overcame prejudices and recognized the Body of Christ as a whole.

The Apostle Paul wrote much about the Body of Christ, the Church.

Now I plead with you, brethren, by the name of our Lord Jesus Christ, that you all speak the same thing, and that there be no divisions among you, but that you be perfectly joined together in the same mind and in the same judgment (1 Corinthians 1:10).

Then in chapter twelve he writes more specifically,

For as the body is one and has many members, but all the members of that one body, being many, are one body, so also is Christ. For by one Spirit we were all baptized into one body — whether Jews or Greeks, whether slaves or free — and have all been made to drink into one Spirit (1 Corinthians 12:12-13).

One of our visiting lecturers was an Orthodox Jew from Jerusalem who had become a Christian believer. A Christian woman from Finland had witnessed to him while touring the Holy Land. He was quite attracted to her but also disturbed by her witness. He began to search through his Jewish Torah for references to the Messiah. The more diligent he was in his quest the more convinced he became that Jesus truly was the Promised Messiah of the Torah. He trusted in Jesus and found the reality that he longed for. Our students and faculty loved to sit under his teaching on the Jewish feasts and how they related to our Christian faith.

While living in Sri Lanka, I was privileged to dedicate the first church among the Birhor people in Bihar with N.J. Varughese. We were also invited by A. Stephen and his wife, Queeny, to dedicate his headquarters' church in Bangalore, south central India. Pattie was pregnant with Nathan at the time. It was really hot and uncomfortable for her to travel, but

God gave her grace. Courageously she was determined to make the trip with me.

I had sold my car a few years before meeting Pattie and sent money for Stephen to purchase windows and ceiling fans for the new church. They were delighted that Pattie and I were close by in Sri Lanka, just a two hour flight away. Their home was like our home. A couple of years later they and their family visited us in Sri Lanka. Our home was like their home. This is a true picture of the Family of God.

I had seen the American brand of popular Christianity exulting notoriety, wealth, multi-million dollar buildings and expansion projects and a celebrity circuit of preachers and Christian entertainers. Pioneer church-planting leaders with whom we were associated in India and Sri Lanka were more concerned with soul winning, training ministers, and planting churches where there were no churches – where Jesus was not known.

I became painfully aware of some glaring discrepancies between what we Americans say we believe as Christians and what we actually do. I was struck by the statement of an English atheist who said, "If I believed what you Christians say you believe, that man's eternal destiny lies with his choice to receive or reject the Lord Jesus Christ, I would crawl on my hands and knees clear across England on broken glass just to tell one soul." I do not know if he was truthful about that, but he had the right slant toward dedication to the Christian faith.

The Bible says that Jesus came to seek and to save the lost (Matthew 19:10). In Romans 3:23 it says, *for all have sinned and fall short of the glory of God.* Romans 6:23 clarifies the human condition even more. *For the wages of sin is death, but the gift of God is eternal life in Christ Jesus our Lord.* Jesus never appeared frenetic over the depravity of man, but he was always reaching out to save anyone who was ready to repent. The Lord recognized the world His Father had sent Him to as a fallen world with a lost humanity desperately needing salvation.

Jesus showed immeasurable compassion for the multitudes which he saw as sheep without a shepherd (Matthew 9:35-36). At the same time He reached out to a diminutive and despised tax collector who had shimmied up a sycamore tree to get a glimpse of Him as He passed by (Luke 19:1-10). He was never hurried but always determined and destined to reach somebody, someplace.

Jesus was a Man with a mission. A Man on the move. For example, as He ministered to people and preached the Good News, some fans tried to keep Him from leaving them. He said to them,

I must preach the kingdom of God to the other cities also, because for this purpose I have been sent (Luke 4:43).

Many of the villages we were reaching in the Indian interior did not have electricity. Most people were just subsisting. Their whole life seemed like a struggle just to survive. Americans have so much compared to these people. I discovered that we have about 6% of the world's population and yet control the vast majority of the world's wealth. I was very disturbed to learn that out of the total American church budget less than one percent was allocated to reach people who have not yet heard the Gospel message. This is unthinkable if we really believe that man is eternally lost without Jesus Christ.

Why should some hear the Gospel over and over when many on this planet have never heard it for the first time? Are a few American souls more valuable than a multitude of poor Indian villagers or Stone Age tribal people in the deep Amazon jungle? What we truly believe, I concluded, is proved by the way we spend our time and money. The average American church needs to repent and do what God has called them to do.

Pattie, the boys, and I stopped in Hong Kong on one of our trips. We visited Pastor Balcom, an American who pastors a church there. He gave us a video of the underground church in China which he had produced after visiting many house churches throughout the country. I was deeply moved by what I saw. Chinese believers clandestinely worshipped and prayed in packed rooms. Tears were streaming down many faces intense in prayer. When I asked why they were praying with such emotion, Pastor Balcom solemnly told me they were praying for the American church!

I saw these praying saints in China as the hidden gems of the Church. When Peter pointed out to Jesus that they had left everything to follow Him, the Lord answered that they would receive a hundred fold in this life *But many who are first will be last, and the last first* (Mark 10:31). Jesus made this statement in reference to sacrifice, suffering, and Kingdom investment. The Chinese intercessors are part of the hidden family in the Body of Christ who I believe will be among the honored first at judgment.

As missionaries, we were keenly aware of our family of prayer partners and supporters. They were and are the life-line of our ministry. All are not in a position to go, but prayer partners can pray. They can give. God sees their faithfulness even if they are unrecognized in this life. We have had prayer warriors and supporters who depend on their social security and yet faithfully donate to us. We support others in turn.

One couple signed up to receive my mission newsletter when I first went to India. They faithfully prayed for two years and began to feel a burden to go to India themselves. They were accepting God's call to an extreme adventure. Richard Kiser accompanied me to India on one of my trips. There God confirmed his call. Subsequently he and his wife, Betty, sold their home, took early retirement from his job, and submitted their passports to the Indian Embassy for missionary visas. I had doubts that their applications would be approved, but in their late fifties they were set to go.

A few months later I knocked on their door. I had been praying for them but still had no assurance that this would work out. Looking at Richard's face I knew the answer. Glumly he pointed to an end table across the room. Two dark blue American passports were laying next to an antique lamp. The official Indian government stamp said "Rejected." India was not open to accept new missionary visas.

There was a long period of silence. Richard's head was still bowed in dejection as he sat in his lounge chair. "Richard," I said, "do you know that thirty miles off the southeast coast of India is an island country called Sri Lanka? It used to be called Ceylon until 1972 when it adopted a new constitution." I told him about the retirement scheme that the Sri Lankan government had created for expatriates to live on the island. "You can easily fly back and forth to India from there," I reassured him.

Richard's countenance immediately changed. He was uplifted with the news. When God truly gives you a vision, He will give you the provision to accomplish it. The Kisers spent many fruitful years there. Hundreds of churches under the banner of The Four Square Gospel Church are now scattered throughout the country.

One rural Indiana church closed and sold the property. The church board decided to give the proceeds to build an orphanage in Orissa, India. An Indian friend went to visit Richard and Betty and stayed in their home for several months while Richard helped him organize the Orissa Project. Richard knew that I had little time but wanted me to become the first President since I was the initiator of the contact. Reluctantly I accepted the position, but he did all the work as Secretary-Treasurer. Happy Valley Children's Home continues to help poor rural children in the hill country of that state. Again only God knows the hidden Family of God who made this all possible.

Pattie and I agreed that our sons, Nathan and Timmy, needed the opportunity to finish their education in America and get established there if they so desired. Our return to the states was for them. They had grown much in understanding community while living in a multi-national boarding school. They made friends from many countries such as Mauritius, New Zealand, Australia, Malaysia, Myanmar, Sweden, and, of course, India and Sri Lanka, and even many tribal people. Just living in India was an education in itself. They learned vital lessons being separated from Mom and Dad. God blessed them with this wonderful opportunity to grow as citizens of the world.

The 1981 Academy Award winning motion picture, *Chariots of Fire*, was based on the true story of a missionary to China, Eric Lidell, who was also an Olympic champion runner in the 1920s. In his early running career his missionary sister was fearful that his seriousness about competitive running would interfere with their work in China.

He pleaded for her understanding with this penetrating affirmation, "My dear sister, when I run, I feel the favor of God." He never compromised his convictions and abstained from competing on Sunday. He went on to win a gold medal in another event that was not his specialty. God honored him. Years later Lidell was killed by the Communists while serving in China.

In late summer of 1996 we were checking in at the Bandaranaika International Airport in Sri Lanka. We were headed back to the USA for another phase of this extreme adventure. As customs inspectors rummaged through our luggage, a familiar melody lifted our heads. The terminal sound system was playing our adopted family theme song, *Chariots of Fire*. What a coincidence! I glanced at Nathan and Timmy and raised my clinched fist in the air. We had made it our family custom to do that whenever we heard this inspiring instrumental. They stood there grinning and shaking their heads in wonder. God was sending us home for a time but not without a plan. What was our next step? The extreme adventure is a moment by moment walk, one step at a time.

> *As you therefore have received Christ Jesus the Lord, so walk in Him* (Colossians 2:6).

Sometimes our extreme adventures include pain. The boys had suffered in India. Timmy was hospitalized for ten days. Thirteen bottles of glucose slowly dripped into his veins to relieve his dehydration. He had lost most of his body fat and was very frail. Nathan had also become very thin and listless with a persistent cough. Overall they cherish their experience in India. They vividly remember those days and are thankful for the opportunity that was given to them. They talk about someday returning and touring all over India on a motorcycle. Our graduation present to each of them was a return trip to India and Sri Lanka, but they want to go again on their own. I think Asia is in their blood.

We were leaving Sri Lanka but not without a vision and plan. Through extended times of prayer, worship, and fasting Pattie and I became sensitive to what the Spirit was saying. Acts 13:2-3 says,

> As they ministered to the Lord and fasted, the Holy Spirit said, "Now separate to Me Barnabas and Saul for the work to which I have called them." Then, having fasted and prayed, and laid hands on them, they sent them away.

God gave us a vision for Sri Lanka and Lanka Bible College. We would have a Prayer Tower on our campus. It was actually a World Missions Prayer Center. I clearly saw in my mind the island geographically formed like praying hands. Light was shining out of the finger tips up into India and the band of nations missiologists refer to as the 10/40 Window. These are the nations from North Africa to Southeast Asia where most of the unevangelized peoples of the world live.

The Prayer Center was to be constructed with a reddish tile roof in an octagonal shape in Sri Lankan architectural form and fashion. Inside the two-story structure I envisioned a prayer chapel with a lighted hanging globe suspended from the ceiling. Bulletin boards with up-to-date prayer requests and reports from around the world would be placed on the walls.

In the Spirit I envisioned students receiving instruction on the 10/40 Window and looking intently at maps and praying over them. In the spirit we saw teams going throughout Sri Lanka teaching in churches offering practical information about prayer and world missions and exhorting believers to become world intercessors just as the Christians in China. We believed that literally millions would be saved as a result of the prayer generated from here either directly or indirectly. In our vision we saw churches coming together in this special place of prayer. Intercession and world evangelism is something all believers can agree on.

Unity was a strong emphasis of Dr. E. Stanley Jones who urged the union of a Federation of Churches in his autobiography entitled *Song of Ascents*. He touched my life deeply with his emphasis on the Kingdom of God. I was also privileged to spend a few hours alone with David du Plessis five months before he went to be with the Lord. David was known throughout Christendom as 'Mr. Pentecost.' His tireless work to bring Protestants and Roman Catholics together was remarkable. He was a true Christian ecumenist. Both of these men of God had influenced my thinking on church unity and God's Kingdom, so it was not surprising that these emphases were part of our vision for the Prayer Tower on campus.

We have been fortunate and blessed to have Kingdom-thinking men of God as our pastors in America. While we lived in the Ft. Worth area, Pastor Des Evans of Bethesda Community Church captured our hearts with his stirring messages and inspired praying from the pulpit. He prayed for the churches in the area by name because he had a relationship with them. I had not heard a pastor do that before on a regular basis. When we moved again God led us to Covenant Church and Pastor Mike Hayes. The international and interracial mix of Covenant Church along with his revelatory teaching and the anointed worship made us feel right at home. Both of these churches laid hands on us and sent us out when we moved away from their communities. Both pray for and support us today. We are grateful for all that these men, their wives, staff, and congregations have invested in us.

The vision we had for Sri Lanka and Lanka Bible College Prayer Tower was so clear and exciting that we could not keep it to ourselves. The first person we shared it with was the college principal, Ben Manikam. He wholeheartedly agreed. "It is from the Lord, Terry. It is only a matter of God's timing." There were other building projects already under construction or on the drawing board. The Prayer Tower would become a reality in God's time, but the prayer ministry, Brother Ben noted, could begin now with or without the prayer center. With his leadership and support it did.

Pattie and I invested the initial gift to construct the steep walkway up the hill to the auditorium and prospective site. Months later it was a profound encouragement for our faith to see the steps reaching to the top of the hill. With our spirits we also could see the Prayer Tower. It would be a "house of prayer for all nations" as Jesus called the cleansed temple (Mark 11:17 and Isaiah 56:7). In the meantime the physical aspect of the vision would have to wait.

At the same time the Holy Spirit urged us to put the vision on paper.

Then the LORD answered me and said: "Write the vision and make it plain on tablets, that he may run who reads it. For the vision is yet for an appointed time; but at the end it will speak, and it will not lie. Though it tarries, wait for it; because it will surely come, It will not tarry (Habakkuk 2:2-3).

We designed a brochure with expert help from Christian printers in the capital city. These we carried with us to the USA. We mailed them to our prayer partners who began to stand with us for the vision to become a reality. The seed was planted.

We had sought the Lord for our next step upon leaving the island. He had not disappointed us. Others believed in our report, especially our Sri Lankan pastors, Rev. Dr. Varghese Chandy, and his wife,Hildagaard, who were the founders of Lanka Bible College and later New Covenant Church in Colombo.

In the meantime I continued to minister God's Word in India, Sri Lanka, Malaysia, Australia, and wherever God opened doors. In the USA I challenged believers to *look at the fields, for they are already white for harvest* (John 4:35). We considered America a mission field too. Nathan and Timmy were part of a post Christian generation in which the church seemed irrelevant. God would have to sovereignly move in the hearts of America's youth and young adults. Only He could penetrate this spiritual darkness. We believe it will happen!

Seven years after the initial distribution of those Prayer Tower brochures, I received a call from one of our prayer partners. He lived in the Dallas area and asked me to come see him. I sat with him on his living room floor. Jim Yarborough poured out his story. Their twenty-six year old son, Paul, had died in a car crash, killed instantly on a Dallas freeway. "Satan," he said, "took my dear son out of this world too early in life. The devil has to pay. Millions of Christian reapers are going to be released into the harvest fields of South Asia." Paul's death would not be in vain.

Jim informed me that he had carried the Prayer Tower brochure in his Bible for more than three years. Our vision had become his vision. He then told me that the insurance money received from Paul's death would be used to build The Prayer Tower of Sri Lanka. He and Sarah, his wife, and the principal of Lanka Bible College were committed to go ahead with the project. In October of 2003 the beautiful new building was dedicated and is now in use, open to all church groups on the island and visiting groups from abroad as well.

A year after Paul's untimely death, Satan tried to take out our oldest son Nathan. I was returning from India and landed at Dallas International Airport. One of our dear prayer partners met me. After I sat down in his car he said, "We have to go to the Methodist Hospital. Your son, Nathan, had an accident last night and is in the intensive care." My heart sank.

At the hospital I learned that he had been a passenger on a motorcycle that crashed near our home. The paramedic team could not get him to respond, so they called in a helicopter to fly him to the nearest hospital. He had a broken collar bone and head traumas because he had not been wearing a helmet. He regained consciousness but suffered a broken hand and wrist that required surgery and insertion of a metal plate. God touched him and continues to heal him in every way.

Weeks later we received an email from one of our missionary prayer partners in the jungle border between Venezuela and Colombia. Bruce Olson and the Motilone tribe were praying for Nathan. Bruce was the missionary anthropologist whom I had gotten to know and love after he stayed with me for a week in the mid-seventies. His story is well documented in the best-selling book, *Bruchko*, published by Charisma House.

When he was just nineteen years old, God led him into these border jungles to contact the fierce Motilone tribe. He wanted to communicate the Gospel of Jesus Christ. His first contact was a four-foot arrow shot into his hip, but five years later Bobi became his first convert. Today the Motilone are Christians and reach out to other tribes with the Gospel message.

In 1989 I met Bruce again in Pittsburg, Pennsylvania, at a mission's conference held in a hotel near the airport. He invited me up to his room for lunch. There he told me personally what I had already read in the *Readers Digest*. The communist guerrilla movement had taken him captive and held him for nine months hoping to coerce him into joining their cause. He was put before a firing squad as a last resort by the commander who happened to be an ex-Roman Catholic priest. When the shots rang out and the smoke cleared, Bruce stood there without a blindfold, unscathed, staring at his would-be executioners.

The commander advanced to face Bruce half grinning with the reason for the apparent miracle. He admitted he had placed blanks in the carbines during the night. The Motilone elders, contrary to what Bruce was told by the commander for months, had been lobbying for his safe return. They had resolutely told the communist leaders that if Bruce Olson was killed, they would go to war with the communists. The commander freely admitted that they did not want another war front and had probably made a mistake by taking Bruce hostage in the first place. Soon thereafter they released him to return to the tribe.

These *Bari* people were initially Stone Age brothers and sisters in Christ but now have made great advancements in their jungle communities which center on their belief in God manifested as the Word become flesh.

We keep in touch with Bruce through our I AM newsletters and send him support through our church. He also sends his newsletters to us and occasionally writes personal notes.

I quote from his March, 2006, letter. "The Bari say 'violence engenders violence,' and will not take bow and arrow against intruders." He continues, "Chieftains of the Ichirringdacayra Convention determine to continue to live their vow . . . emulate compassion as experienced in the death and resurrection of Jesus Christ. As God became incarnate in human flesh in the life of Jesus, live His example in the 21st Century, and . . . trust Him for protection." God is using this tribe to witness to the eighteen isolated tribal peoples of northeast Colombia, an estimated population of 350,000 (many situated in the non-explored border areas common with Venezuela).

In February, 2006, Pattie and I saw *End of the Spear*, a movie that depicted the true story of the five American missionaries who were killed by the Auca Indians in the deep jungles of Ecuador in the mid fifties. The narrative is told from the view point of Steve Saint, the pilot's son who has since returned with his family to live among the tribe that killed his father. The Indian man who actually speared his dad to death is now a grandfather and the surrogate grandfather also to Steve Saint's children. We were so inspired by this movie that we invited many people and eventually saw it three times ourselves. God's family is awesome!

Rousseau's concept of the noble savage is certainly an illusion. The Auca tribe would now be extinct if those five missionaries and their families had not followed the Lord and laid down their lives to bring them the Good News. Inter-tribal warfare had greatly diminished their population. There were no grandfathers before Jesus came to them. For the first time the men are living long enough to see their grandchildren. Now they are making great advancements and learning how to adapt to a modern world which is quickly closing in on them.

Many years ago Bruce Olson was invited by the late renowned anthropologist Margaret Mead to lecture in her classes at Columbia University. When he finished, she stammered somewhat angrily blurting out, "Bruce Olson, all you have done is to make these Motilones a bunch of little Jesus Christs." He thanked her and sat down. Bruce and Steve Saint had answered the query posed by Richard on the UCLA campus in the mid-nineteen sixties. The human race is lost and without hope outside of Jesus Christ, whether it is in New York City, a little burg called Seaville, New Jersey, or the deep jungles of the Amazon. Man is separated from

God unless he has a relationship with the resurrected Jesus Christ.

After Pentecost Peter and John prayed for a lame man and he was healed. They also preached and taught about Jesus as being the fulfillment of the Old Covenant prophecies. This so disturbed the Jewish religious authorities that they were arrested and interrogated.

> *"By what power or by what name have you done this?" Then Peter, filled with the Holy Spirit, said to them, "Rulers of the people and elders of Israel: If we this day are judged for a good deed done to a helpless man, by what means he has been made well, let it be known to you all, and to all the people of Israel, that by the name of Jesus Christ of Nazareth, whom you crucified, whom God raised from the dead, by Him this man stands here before you whole. This is the 'stone which was rejected by you builders, which has become the chief cornerstone.' Nor is there salvation in any other, for there is no other name under heaven given among men by which we must be saved" Acts 4:7b-12).*

Bruce Olson was nineteen years old when he left his family and home in Minneapolis, Minnesota to take the Good News of Jesus Christ to a Stone Age tribe. More than 40 years later, he still lives with the Motilone and assists them in their outreaches to fifty other tribes with various social projects. They are a brilliant shining example of the power of God to transform a whole nation.

Epologue

In the Spring of 2006, Pattie and I visited our friends in Nagaland, northeast India. Sister Alila Vito is the Director of Christ for the Nations Bible College of Nagaland. It was then we learned that the Naga's have sixteen tribes speaking nine distinct languages scattered across the mountain forests of far northeast India.

One hundred years ago they were warring among themselves and their neighbors. They believed that an enemy's head hung outside the home brought respect to their household. Today most of the Nagas consider themselves Christians and many Naga missionaries have even been sent out to other people groups and countries.

While at the college we met students from Assam, Myanmar , Nepal, and several of the Naga tribes. The chapel services were very lively and joyful with harmonizing in different languages and dialects. It was exactly what I expect heaven's singing to sound like.

They showed their love to us with the gift of a special hand-made, shell embroidered vest which I am wearing in the picture on the back cover. Our plans for the years ahead are to help the Nagas in their future missionary endeavors to neighboring tribes and countries.

From Nagaland we went on to visit our brothers and sisters in Jharkand (formerly southern Bihar). N. J. Varughese and Joycutty started the Christian work there in the early seventies. Now there are over two hundred churches, a training center, a mobile medical center, an orphanage, and over four hundred evangelists and church planters. Ground was broken to begin construction of a modern, seventy-five bed clinic and future hospital in a tribal area of the state. Varughese told us that there would always be a place for Pattie and me to reside in their hospital community and compound. If the Lord does not return before I die, that is where I plan to spend my last days, teaching and ministering God's word and His love.

Continuing south we were blessed once again to be with A. Stephen and his wife, Queeny, in Bangalore. Currently they are constructing a much needed orphanage next to their beautiful campus and World Prayer Center. Pattie and I prayed there for hours and enjoyed a special presence of the Lord. Cornerstone Ministries of India, which Stephen established after leaving OM, has planted hundreds of churches and built a modern, thirty-bed hospital where Jesus Christ is shared along with excellent medical treatment.

It was a joy to cross the straits to visit our Sri Lankan family as well. Our lives are intertwined with many precious servants of the Lord in South Asia and we expect *Extreme Adventure* to widen our family circle even more. Will you join us? Will you help us spread the word?

I trust that you have been inspired by reading *Extreme Adventure,* but that has not been my main purpose in writing it. If you have been affected emotionally and miss the reality of actually becoming involved in the Kingdom of God that Jesus emphasized, you have missed the point. I have endeavored to be simple and straight-forward, knowing that my efforts and aspirations fall far short of perfect communication. In the process I have birthed a close semblance of what our Father put in my heart and is working within us even today.

I would be amiss if I did not offer you some tangible means to respond to what I have written, to actually tie your ship to the Lord's dock, and then to sail the high seas in the Lord's service in these last days. Yes, these are the last days. You have not read this book by coincidence. Now is your time. We have all been living on borrowed time.

> *The Lord is not slow in keeping His promise, as some understand*
> *slowness. He is patient with you, not wanting anyone to perish,*
> *but everyone to come to repentance* (2 Peter 3:9).

James, the brother of Jesus who initially did not believe in Him as the Messiah but later became a pillar in the early Church in Jerusalem, provokes us all to consider our priorities in the light of life's brevity.

> *Why, you do not even know what will happen tomorrow. What is*
> *your life? You are a mist that appears for a little while and then*
> *vanishes* (James 4:14).

The Kingdom of God requires that we accept Him as King and the true Sovereign. What He commands, we as His subjects are obliged to do. In this age of terrorism His Word remains the standard. If many people's love for God is growing cold as wickedness intensifies (Matthew 24:12), we must remain hot in our faith. We must persevere in doing our part to take the Gospel to *all nations*. The Father has chosen weak human vessels to spread His Word. That is the way it is! He is not writing love letters in the sky. He is sending His disciples as His living epistles – communicating Christ-like love manifested through real skin and bone.

We must not presume that just because we are saved and satisfied, we have no responsibility to see that every nation is represented around the throne of God. We must not presume that it is *not* our calling to be involved in someway. If this is God's priority on planet Earth (as He said it is), then each one of His subjects ought to be enthused with His passion for the nations.

We can be so consumed with our immediate surroundings, our rightful mission field, that we are unresponsive to His plan for the nations. On the other hand we might be so focused on the nations that we neglect the present mission field where God has placed us. It is not an either/or issue. We are not to be *conformed to this world* (Romans 12:2), but we are called to be world Christians. We are to be knowledgeable of our brothers and sisters around the world and the mission fields they present to us. We are to be involved in some significant manner through prayer, giving, and spreading the world vision, and if God calls, to go ourselves.

The Holy Spirit will lead you. Of this I am certain. He will lead each of us to be an integral part of a local Body of Believers, the Church. Pattie and I have had the covering of a local church in the USA or overseas ever since we were married. Before moving to a new location we first of all found a church home in the vicinity. Then we were sent out with the blessing of our elders and covering church to our new church home. We are blessed to have the continued support of those former home-base churches.

Have you noticed the harvest field that surrounds you? In John 4:35b Jesus speaks:

Open your eyes and look at the fields! They are ripe for harvest.

That is something you can see right where you are. Our Father has brought the nations to us in America. Indians and other Asians, Mexicans, and tribal peoples are living among us. In fact people from most nations are living among us. You can befriend them and share the love of Jesus. One of our dear pastor friends has an effective outreach to the Navajo Nation in Arizona. They need the Lord too!

There are many mission organizations with which you can become involved. In this book I have mentioned Operation Mobilization, All India Mission with N. J. Varughese, Cornerstone Ministries in India with A. Stephen, Lanka Bible College, and other missions in Sri Lanka, and Bruce Olson and his work among the Motilones in South America. Youth with a Mission (YWAM) also offers a variety of opportunities to fulfill your world-wide vision. These are just a few that we have been personally connected to over the years. Check with your pastor for others affiliated with your church.

Again, I want to reiterate that God will lead you by His Spirit. We are all unique individuals with our own special DNA. Pattie and I will pray for you. You can contact us through our website: www.impactasiaministries.com or our mission's office: International Missions Network, P.O. Box 110099, Carrollton, Texas 75011-0099. You may order more books by emailing me at terroljones@comcast.net. Will you help us pass this challenge to your friends, relatives, and acquaintances?

Proceeds from the sale of this book will help support missionaries around the world. We plan to take this message to college campuses throughout the USA and wherever God opens the doors. We can do this with your help.

We believe that thousands will accept the challenge and become true world Christians. Will you believe with us? You can also be part of our I AM (Impact Asia Ministries) family by receiving our newsletter. We hope to hear from you. We pray that you are enjoying your Extreme Adventure with the Lord right now.

> *And without faith it is impossible to please God, because anyone who comes to him must believe that he exists, and that he rewards those who earnestly seek him* (Hebrews 11:6).

We have been immeasurably rewarded by placing our faith unreservedly in Him. Being committed to His Kingdom building and plan for the nations means truly marching to the beat of a Different Drummer. The world system is now espousing an age of extremes. Many are dedicating themselves to the extreme of terrorism.

Christian believers need to hear what the Spirit of God is saying. Only Jesus Christ offers the real extreme adventure which He made fully available for us on the cross. There is not only a distinct rhythm in the march through life with Jesus, but a lovely inner symphony of wholeness, peace, and satisfaction with God. The counterfeits offered by the world system will never make you complete as a person. That comes only in loving the Lord and seeking to follow Him, holding nothing back.

God continues to call His children to this extreme adventure. Jesus often said, *If any man has ears to hear, let him hear.* (Matthew 11:15) Do you hear the beat? Has His heavenly symphony captured your imagination?

> *Your ears shall hear a word behind you, saying 'This is the way, walk in it,' Whenever you turn to the right hand or whenever you turn to the left* (Isaiah 30:21).

Your Comments are appreciated:
   Write to Terrol Jones
   P.O.Box 124
   Ocean City, NJ 08226

BIBLIOGRAPHY

Carothers, Merlin. *Prison to Praise*. Escondido: Merlin Carothers, 1970.

Colson, Charles. *How Now Shall We Live*. Wheaton: Tyndale House, 1999.

Deer, Jack. *Surprised By The Power Of The Spirit,* Grand Rapids: Zondervan, 1993.

DuPlessis, David. *Simple and Profound*. New Orleans: Paraclete Press, 1986.

Gospel Literature Service, Editors. *Burnt Alive*. Mumbai, India: GLS, 1999.

Hesssion, Roy. *Calvary Road*. Ft. Washington, PA: Christian Literature Crusade, 1964

Jones, E. Stanley. *Song of Ascents: A Spiritual Autobiography*. Nashville: Abington, 1968.

_____. *Victory Through Surrender*. Nashville: Abington, 1971.

Lewis, C. S. *Mere Christianity*. London: C. S. Lewis Private Ltd, 1952

McDonald, William. *True Discipleship*. Kansas City: Walterick Publishers, 1975.

Murray, Andrew. *Absolute Surrender*. Gainsville: Bridge-Hogas, 2005.

Narayan, M.R. *Inside an Illusive Mind - Prabakaran*. Colombo, Sri Lanka: Vijithi Yapa, 2003.

Nee, Watchman. *The Spiritual Man* (V1-3). New York: Christian Fellowship Publishers, 1977.

Olson, Bruce. *For This Cross I'll Kill You (* renamed *Bruchko)*. Lake Mary, FL: Charisma House, 1976.

Piper, John. *The Passion of Jesus Christ*. Wheaton: Crossway Books, 2003.

Schaeffer, Francis A. *How Shall We Then Live*. Westchester: Crossway Books, 1976.

Sjogren, Bob. *Unveiled At Last*. Seattle: YWAM Publishing, 1992.

Tozer, A. W. *Of God and Man*. Harrisburg, PA: Christian Publications, 1960.

Varughese, Ellen. *The Freedom To Marry*. Olathe, KS: Joy Press, 1992.

Warren, Rick. *The Purpose Driven Life*. Grand Rapids: Zondervan, 2002.

Whyte, H. A. Maxwell. *The Power of the Blood*. New Kensington, PA: Whitaker House, 1973

APPENDIX

You may contact these ministries directly:

All India Mission, Brother N. J. Varughese: allindiacgm@gmail.com

Asbury Theological Seminary: www.asburytheologicalseminary.org

Campus Crusade for Christ: www.campuscrusadeforchrist.com

Cornerstone Ministries in India with Brother A. Stephen:
stephen@blr.vsnl.net.in

Hope for Asia with Dr. Varghese Chandy: Anchor Bay Evangelistic
Association, P.O. Box 406 Maryville, IL 62062-0406 or
joyvision@hotmail.com

Impact Asia Ministries with Terrol and Pattie Jones:
www.impactasiaministries.com or
terryjones@impactasiaministries.com

India Evangelistic Association with Pran Parrichhua in Orissa:
iea_prp@hotmail.com

Lanka Bible College, The Principal, P.O. Box 2, Peradeniya, Sri Lanka
or % of Anchor Bay Evangelistic Association, P.O. Box 406,
Maryville, IL 62062-0406

Lanka Ministries International, Anton George: antnlmi@hotmail.com

Motilone tribe of South America with Bruce Olson:
www.bruceolson.org or 7543 NW 70 Street, Miami, FL 33166
or Apartado 1808, Bucaramagna, Columbia

Nagaland: Christ for the Nations, P.O.Box 26, Kohima, Nagaland,
India 797001 or alilavito@yahoo.co.in

Operation Mobilization: www.usa.om.org

Youth with a Mission (YWAM): www.ywam.org